D0558115

You're in Charge!

A Guide to Becoming Your Own Therapist

International College—"the College that's reviving the tutor-student tradition"—was founded in 1970 as a viable alternative to traditional higher education. Over 150 tutors, many of them world-renowned, engage in the learning process with students on a one-to-one or small-group basis. For information, write to International College, 1019 Gayley Avenue, Los Angeles, CA 90024, or call (213) 477-6761.

Guild of Tutors Press is the publishing arm of International College. See page 223 for other books published by the Guild of Tutors Press.

You're In Charge!

A Guide to Becoming Your Own Therapist

Janette Rainwater, Ph.D.

Cover by Corita Kent

International College

Guild of Tutors Press

Los Angeles

You're In Charge! A Guide to Becoming Your Own Therapist.
Copyright © 1979, by Janette Rainwater. All rights reserved. Printed
in the United States of America. No part of this book may be used
or reproduced in any manner whatsoever without written permission
except for brief quotations embodied in critical articles or reviews.
For information, address: Guild of Tutors Press, International College,
1019 Gayley Avenue, Los Angeles, California 90024. (213/477-6761)

FIRST EDITION

10 9 8 7 6 5 4 3 2 1

Library of Congress Catalog Number 79-65000

ISBN 0-89615-021-6

Designed by Paul O. Proehl

Grateful acknowledgment is made to the following for permission to reprint material
from:

The Female Eunuch by Germaine Greer. Copyright © 1970 by Germaine Greer. Used
with permission of Mc-Graw-Hill Book Company. / *Zen in the Art of Archery* by
Eugen Herrigel. Copyright © 1953 by Pantheon Books, Inc. Reprinted by permission
of Pantheon Books, a Division of Random House, Inc. / *This Timeless Moment* by
Laura Huxley. Copyright © 1968 by Laura Huxley. Reprinted by permission of
Celestial Arts, Millbrae, California / *Journey of a Dream Animal* by Kathleen Jenks.
Copyright © 1975 by Kathleen Jenks. Used by permission of the Julian Press, a
division of Crown Publishers, Inc. / *Memories, Dreams, Reflections* by C.G. Jung;
recorded and edited by Aniela Jaffe; translated by Richard and Clara Winston. Copy-
right © 1961 by Random House, Inc. Reprinted by permission of Pantheon Books,
a Division of Random House, Inc. / *Gestalt Therapy Verbatim* by Frederick S. Perls.
Copyright © 1969 by Real People Press. Reprinted by permission of Real People
Press, Moab, Utah. / *In and Out the Garbage Pail* by Frederick S. Perls. Copyright ©
1969 by Real People Press. Reprinted by permission of Real People Press, Moab,
Utah. / "the lady with the braid" by Dory Previn. Copyright © 1971 by Dory Previn.
Quoted with permission of Dory Previn. / *Rilke on Love and Other Difficulties,
Translations and Considerations of Rainer Maria Rilke*, by John J. L. Mood, with the
permission of W. W. Norton & Company, Inc. Copyright © 1975 by W. W. Norton
& Company, Inc. / *Jung and the Story of Our Time* by Laurens van der Post. Copyright © 1975 by Laurens van der Post. Reprinted by permission of Pantheon Books,
a Division of Random House, Inc. / *The Diary of Anaïs Nin*, Volume II, by Anaïs Nin.
Copyright © 1967 by Anaïs Nin. Reprinted by permission of Harcourt Brace Jovanovich, Inc. / *The Teachings of Ramana Maharishi*. Reprinted by permission of the
publisher, Samuel Weiser, Inc. / *Social Readjustment Rating Scale* used with permission
of Thomas H. Holmes, M.D., University of Washington School of Medicine, Department
of Psychiatry and Behavioral Sciences, Seattle. / *Fear of Flying* by Erica Jong. © 1973
by Erica Mann Jong. Excerpts from pages 314-15 reprinted by permission of Holt, Rinehart and Winston. / *The Book of Secrets* by Bhagwan Shree Rajneesh. © 1974 by the
Rajneesh Foundation. Excerpts from Vol. I, p. 216, reprinted by permission of Harper
& Row. / *Island* by Aldous Huxley. © 1962 by Aldous Huxley. Excerpt from page 268
reprinted by permission of Harper & Row. / "Anatomy of an Illness as Perceived by
the Patient," *New England Journal of Medicine*, Vol. 295, No. 26, p. 1458-63. © 1976
by Norman Cousins. Reprinted by permission of Norman Cousins.

CONTENTS

Foreword / 7

1. Introduction: The Art of Self Observation / 9

2. Games People Play in Their Heads:
   Constructive and Destructive Uses of Fantasy / 13

3. You're in Charge of Your Personal Relationships:
   Getting Along with Other People / 50

4. On Keeping a Journal / 92

5. The Uses of Autobiography / 99

6. On Dreaming / 115

7. Meditation: What, Why, When, and How / 138

8. Awareness and the Art of Being in the Now / 150

9. You're in Charge of Your Physical Health / 163

10. Death (and the Possibility That You're in
    Charge Here, Too!) / 194

Bibliography / 212

Index of Exercises / 217

Index / 218

To my teachers . . .
which means all those who have traveled
the Road with me . . .
family, friends, clients, mentors, students . . .
and most especially . . .
Roberto Assagioli, Alice A. Bailey,
George L. Bitzer, Carolyn Conger,
Florence M. Garrigue, Brugh Joy,
Bob Martin, Jeannette A. Munkittrick,
Fritz Perls, Michael Rainwater,
Francis Israel Regardie, Jim Simkin,
Edith Stauffer, Joseph Wheelwright.

FOREWORD

We are into the dawn of a new era in the evolvement of being more fully human. We are just beginning to realize that human beings can more fully realize their potentials for recreating themselves and the world in which they live. Dr. Rainwater's book is a major ray of light coming from that dawn and promises to increase and expand human consciousness.

Reading her book is like opening up a treasure chest which has been taken for granted, forgotten about, and might even have mistakenly been thought to have belonged to someone else. Now, having accidentally or otherwise found it, having opened it, we find that it is full of new possibilities that were previously outside of our current awareness: new uses for old things, new perspectives for viewing both the old and the new, and a vast array of information for making new discoveries through using ourselves in new ways.

Dr. Rainwater takes the smorgasbord of all emerging ideas of the last thirty-five years relative to evolving change of human beings and their behavior and translates them into understandable, useful, practical, and exciting action for any person who is interested in taking their own growth in their own hands.

Can *WE TAKE CHARGE OF OURSELVES?* Dr. Rainwater's answer is a resounding YES. We can: if we think we can, if we have the information, if we know how to use that information, if we have the courage to risk change, and if we see the possibilities. Her book amply demonstrates, informs, and encourages how all this can happen.

Virginia Satir

CHAPTER 1

INTRODUCTION: THE ART OF SELF OBSERVATION

Possibly you're feeling restless. Or you may feel overwhelmed by the demands of wife, husband, children, or job. You may feel unappreciated by those people closest to you. Perhaps you feel angry that life is passing you by and you haven't accomplished all those great things you had hoped to do. Something feels missing from your life. You were attracted by the title of this book and wish that you really were in charge. What to do?

More dramatically, you may feel that you are falling apart. "Can't" concentrate. "Can't" stop crying. And your appointment with the psychotherapist—the one your best friend recommended—is not until Wednesday at 4. What to do?

This book may have something to offer you, although only you can know—if you're willing to take the time to do the exercises and to agree to the proposed self-examination.

The book is intended for those people who are seriously interested in doing self-therapy, who wish to grow, and who are willing to learn to take responsibility for themselves. I'm not against people seeing psychotherapists (of course not—that's how I make my living); however, I believe that psychotherapy is "successful" only when the clients also start learning to do self-therapy. Think about it: a person spends only one to five hours a week with his therapist out of the one hundred hours plus that he is awake. So if he changes or grows during the short time he spends with the therapist, he *must* be doing something helpful for himself during that much longer non-therapy time.

I will never forget Dorothy, who called me on a Monday in tears and "desperate." The earliest I could see her was late on Thursday. As strongly as I believe in the power of the individual to take charge of her life, I was not prepared for the person who entered my office. She was not crying, not desperate, and she had sorted through the recent, harrowing events of her life. She had also made some decisions about future actions. In other words, she had taken charge. When I asked her how she had done this, particularly in view of her state on Monday, she replied, "I was relieved to know that you could see me and that I wouldn't have to go through this alone any more. I was so impatient for Thursday that I started imagining what you would say, how you would analyze my present situation, and what suggestions you would give me." That's self-therapy!

At best the psychotherapist is an expert, creative catalyst who will accelerate the process of self-therapy. At worst, he increases the dependency and hopeless/helpless feelings of his patients by letting them know either subtly or explicitly that he believes that they "need" him and are incapable of taking charge of their own lives. (I will be mentioning throughout the book those situations and circumstances where I believe individual therapy, group therapy, and sometimes family therapy *would* be advisable.) And if you are currently in therapy, you and your therapist might decide that this book would be a useful adjunct to your therapy.

The basic tool whose use is taught throughout this book is the art of self-observation. Philosophers and mystics, people such as Socrates, Gurdjieff, Krishnamurti, the Buddhists, and Lao Tsu, have all stressed the necessity for self-observation or awareness as the first requirement for becoming enlightened. Self-observation is also the principal road to personal freedom from the various self-torture trips that we humans are so adept at taking. It's important to learn the difference between genuine self-observation and introspection or obsessive, squirrel-cage thinking. Much of the book will be concerned with making this discrimination.

The Two Magic Questions

The "how-to" part of this book is deceptively simple. There are two magic questions that you need to ask yourself. The answers that you generate should provide the guidance that you need.

The first magic question: What is happening *right now?* And this includes:

> What am I doing?
> What am I feeling?
> What am I thinking?
> How am I breathing?

The second magic question: What do I want for myself *in this new moment?* That is, do I want to continue the same doing/thinking/feeling/breathing? Or, do I want to make some changes? Actually, you will make many changes upon becoming aware of what *is* without making a deliberate decision to change. For example, the question to another "Are you aware of your breathing right now?" invariably elicits an instantaneous change. It's as if the question makes her* aware that she is inhibiting a normal, full breathing cycle and allows her body to say "Whew!" in relief, take a deep breath, and then exhale it. And how is *your* breathing right now, after having read this paragraph?

An important therapeutic maxim states: Change occurs when you become what you are, not when you try to become what you are not. Change does not occur by resolves to "do better," by "trying," by demands from authority figures, or by pleading, persuasion, or interpretations from Important Others. Paradoxically, change seems to happen when you have abandoned the chase after what you want to be (or think you should be) and have accepted—and fully experienced—what you are.

The chapters to come will develop different ways for you to ask yourself these two magic questions. As you become aware of what is, and of what you want, you become cognizant of how you're in charge . . . and of all the alternatives, options, and choices that are yours to make.

---

*As a feminist, I don't like using the masculine pronouns to stand for both men and women. As a writer, I don't like the awkwardness of the constructions "he/she," "her/him," "s-he," and so on. In the absence of an acceptable unisex pronoun, I will alternate between masculine and feminine pronouns in my anecdotes that are illustrative of both sexes.

Much of the book consists of exercises that I developed rather spontaneously and intuitively in workshops and classes. My suggestion is that you do each exercise at the time it is proposed. You might want to have a special notebook (preferably bound) in which to record the results of the exercises. You may choose *not* to do the exercises but to continue reading or to close the book and do something else altogether. That's fine. I hope that you will be aware that you are making a choice, that *you're in charge* and perhaps, also, that you can identify the voice within, the subpersonality, that urges you to the course of action you take.

I'd like to caution you, however, that your major discoveries and changes will come from *doing* the exercises rather than just reading about them. What you hear, you're apt to forget. What you see, you may remember. What you do, you understand. And you need to do the things you fear if you want to grow.

My own self-observation at this point as I try to visualize those of you who will embark on this course of self-therapy? Pleasure at having finished this manuscript for you and regret at not being able to know you or to watch and enjoy your progress. Being allowed to observe the growth and discoveries of another is the greatest privilege of being a psychotherapist.

CHAPTER 2

GAMES PEOPLE PLAY IN THEIR HEADS: CONSTRUCTIVE AND DESTRUCTIVE USES OF FANTASY

> Those who do not observe the movements of their own minds must of necessity be unhappy.
> —Marcus Aurelius

Jack Stories

Once upon a time a man driving on a little-traveled road in the desert suddenly had a flat tire. To his consternation, he realized that he had no jack to raise his car and change the tire. Then he remembered he had passed a service station about five miles back, and started walking. And thinking. "You know, way out here in the desert there are no other stations around. If the man who owns it doesn't want to be helpful, there's no other place I can go. I'm really at this guy's mercy. He could skin me good just for lending me a jack so I can change my tire. He could charge me $10 . . . He could charge me $20 . . . He could charge me $50, and there wouldn't be anything I could do about it because I'm just . . . why that S.O.B.! My God, how some people will take advantage of their fellow man!" The man arrives at the service station. The owner comes out and asks in a friendly way, "Hello, what can I do for you?" And our friend shouts, "You can take your goddamned jack and you can shove it!"

This is an exaggeration of how unaware we can be of our thought processes, or of how we take an idea, work it over, elaborate it into a big fantasy, and then act upon our fantasy as if it were reality. This is one of the most destructive uses of fantasy: to put so much energy into a fantasy that it takes on the feel of reality, and then to behave as if it were truly real.

Another common example of a jack story: A man starts wondering if his wife is having an affair. He builds a case about how she *could* be having an affair . . . all her unaccounted-for time, the numerous attractive men that she meets in the course of a day, and so on. Unless he realizes he is doing a "jack story," he may convince himself that she is indeed having an affair, in which case he may then escalate matters by

—accusing her
—going to see a lawyer
—initiating an affair of
his own in "retaliation."

The Self-fulfilling Prophecy

One of the reasons it's so important to identify and then avoid negative fantasies is that any images or mental pictures that you create stay around and produce physical conditions and external actions that correspond to your thoughts and images. An esoteric principle states, energy follows thought. If I visualize myself as being in good health, chances are good that I'm going to be in good health. If I imagine that I will get some dreadful disease, I increase the odds that this will happen. Those kids whose mothers say, "Don't get your feet wet, wear your rubbers or you'll catch cold," are typically the kids in school that catch the most colds. They get an image of themselves as being very vulnerable and then *they* start worrying about whether their feet are wet and if they will catch cold—the "self-fulfilling prophecy." If you believe something will happen, you will consciously and unconsciously act in a way that will help create the prophesied event.

Olivia had always predicted that her husband would leave her after the birth of their second child, because this had been her mother's history. During her second pregnancy (which she wanted and her husband didn't), she became irritable and sexually unavailable at the same time that she was deliberately throwing him into situations with a lonely woman friend. Fortunately for her and their marriage, the husband was as intuitive as he was patient and, knowing of her long-standing prophecy, confronted her with his feelings and his suppositions.

The solution is to learn the art of self-observation. At frequent intervals ask yourself the two magic questions:

1. What is happening right now?

> What am I thinking?
> What am I doing?
> What am I feeling?
> How am I breathing?

Answer these questions as though you were objectively observing another person and able to observe everything going on both inside and outside that person. See if you can observe without condemnation and without emotion. Notice especially how you are breathing.

Had Olivia been practiced in self-observation, she would have realized: "Hey, I'm deciding I feel 'too tired' to go to the theater tonight, to create a situation where Ned and Lillian will go somewhere without me. It sounds like I'm testing them to see whether or not they're attracted to one another and whether they'll act on it. Olivia, you're acting as if you believe Ned really will leave you when this baby is born." With these answers, Olivia would have been ready to answer the second question:

2. What do I want for myself right now?

Sometimes when you find yourself doing a "jack story," you may find it difficult to let go of the internal drama, even though the answer to your second magic question is a firm "Cool it."

In such a case you need to ask yourself: What am I getting for myself out of this jack story? What is my investment in continuing it? You may discover that you enjoy being the center of a melodrama or being a "tragedy queen." Or you may have invested a lot of energy in believing that other people are villains and, therefore, you don't wish to give up this particular story line.

You won't be able to stop thinking about the jack story by willing yourself to stop thinking about it. (You remember the old gag, "I will not think about hippopotamuses, I will not think about hippopotami," and, of course, what you are thinking about *is* a hippopotamus.) In this case you need to divert yourself with a positive substitute.

Diversion Exercise

Deliberately focus your gaze on some object in your environment. Look at it, look at all its aspects, smell it, touch it, lose yourself in it. Describe it as if it were a newly invented object. It could be your thumbnail, a paper clip, or your right shoe. "You are brown, your toes are scuffed, your sole is worn more on the inside edge. I can barely read the writing on your lining," and so on.

If you are currently having difficulty staying away from a jack story, you might want to keep with you some small object that you find fascinating to look at or to feel.

If you allow a thought to stay in your head, if you dwell on it and elaborate on it, then it becomes a fantasy. You can also monitor your thoughts and prevent the growth of what might be a destructive fantasy. For example, when a driver passes a highway accident he might think, "Boy, that's a nasty one, glad it wasn't me. Poor folks," and then go on to a clearly different thought. The next time he passes the spot and remembers the accident he might think, "This is where that accident happened, think I'm going too fast, better slow down," and then go on to another thought.

Some people, however, seem to indulge themselves in spaced-out, unaware thinking, especially while driving the freeways where driving can be fairly automatic, thus leaving the mind free to think of other things. Have you ever had the experience of arriving at your exit and suddenly realizing that you were not aware of passing the last several exits? If so, you experienced what I call the Freeway Blanking Out syndrome.

A businessman who commutes long distances once heard me talk on this topic and then realized that he had been indulging in a recurrent fantasy cued to a certain spot on his daily-traveled highway where he had once seen a particularly nasty collision. For a year he had been elaborating a fantasy of being in a similar accident. He no longer bothered with the messy medical details of his injuries and his lingering death (it had taken him several months to arrive at the definitive version of these), but was now perseverating with the details of how his widow and children would cope on the money from his insurance and the sale of his business. The most amazing part is that he was totally unaware of this fantasy until my talk triggered a recollection; he then realized that he had made several major changes in his business because of his fantasy.

This was a particularly destructive fantasy because it led to business decisions "in anticipation of death" that he probably would not have made otherwise. It's an example of a self-torture trip, which is a fantasy that makes you miserable and unhappy while you're doing it. He was fortunate that he had not yet had the accident for which he was so conscientiously preparing.

39 Self-Torture Trips

1. *Disaster Fantasies.* In addition to highway accidents, the expert self-torturer can plan how terrible it would be if his house burned down, his children were killed, his wife was raped, or he got mugged. Television's preoccupation with violence in recent years has been fostering fear and crime fantasies among its viewers.

A team of noted communication specialists, Gerbner and Gross, contrasted opinions of heavy TV viewers (four or more hours per day) with those of light viewers (two hours or less per day). When asked to estimate their own chances of being involved in some sort of violence during a given week, the heavy viewers were much more likely to pick fearful estimates (such as 50–50 or 1 in 10) rather than the more reasonable estimate of 1 in 100. And the movie industry has been aiding the less imaginative with disaster films such as *Earthquake* and *Jaws*.

Some Californians love to torture themselves with fantasies about earthquakes. That's the time to engage in self-observation and tell oneself, "I'm wondering whether or not we're going to have an earthquake this year and worrying about what to do. I would label this a disaster fantasy. I haven't come up with any new practical ideas about what to do. So it seems I'm just spinning my wheels and making myself miserable. I've gotten myself so anxious I'm not even breathing properly. And it's zero on the Richter scale!" Probably, the disaster fantasy would be dropped for some other line of thought.

2. *The "If-Only-I-Had" Game.* You torture yourself by looking back into the past and wishing you had done this, or had not done that. You think, I wish I had never—

> gotten married
> gotten divorced
> taken this job
> quit school
> started school
> and so on.

Or you think of the things you *might* have done:

> If only I had invested in IBM in 1945!
> If only I had been more (patient, critical, understanding, demanding, etc.) with (the children, my spouse, my parents, etc.).
> If only we had bought some acreage instead of renting.
> And so on.

In this kind of self-torture trip your "critic" subpersonality is demanding that you have a perfect ability to predict the future and then punishes you for your normal human lack of such a talent. In addition, you are not accepting the normal ups and downs of life—experiences that can lead to growth.

3. *Pointing-the-Finger-at-the-Other Game.*

You are

> inconsiderate
> unloving
> uncaring about my feelings
> dishonest
> cruel, and so on.

Look what those sons-of-bitches did to me. First this, then that. This doesn't have to be a recent "injury." Edward is an old man who gets a lot of mileage out of fifty- and sixty-year-old injustices. I call it his "rosary of grievances." He almost literally fingers some beads to make sure he tells all his "poor me" stories either for an audience or to himself. Harboring and energizing long-held resentments can prevent a person from moving constructively in the present.

4. *The Damned-If-You-Do, Damned-If-You-Don't Game of Future Prediction.*

If I do this, then *that* will happen. But if I don't, then this other dreadful thing will happen! Some self-observation here might result in: "Joe, you're trying to crystal-ball the future again. And it's interesting that you're predicting disaster from either action. You're using these dubious predictions as an excuse not to take any action. You could just say, I don't wish to make any decision now, and save yourself all this self-torture."

5. *The Ain't-I-Awful Game.*

Nobody likes me because I'm so

> fat
> thin
> young
> old, and so on.

First of all, have you checked this out? "Nobody likes me" is a rather sweeping statement. (Alarm bells ring in my head whenever I hear someone using the words "nobody," "everybody," "always," or "never.") Who doesn't like you? How do you *know* that certain people don't like you? And is it possible that *you* don't like *you* because you're "too fat," for instance? Any time that you decide in your head that some other person feels a certain way or thinks a certain thought, it would be a good idea to check in with yourself to make sure that it is not YOU who has that feeling or thinks that thought. This is the intuitive wisdom behind the old joke: "Nobody likes me because I'm so gross. And if he did, I wouldn't want to be seen with anybody with such bad taste!"

6. *I-Can't-Possibly-Be-Doing-Everything-Right*, so what have I

> forgotten?
> neglected?
> done wrong?

Someone on this kind of self-torture trip can start to go to the movies to have a good time and suddenly think, "Oh, I'm sure I forgot to lock up the house." She will either worry about it all evening or actually go back and check the locked-up house, thereby making everyone late to the movies.

7. *Competitive and Comparison Trips.*
I'm sure

> the boss likes you better than me
> men find you more attractive
> women find you more attractive
> you're making more money than I am
> you're happier than I am
> you have a better sex life
> And so on.

Experts at this game can focus on some friend or acquaintance who is "doing better" than they are and make themselves quite miserable with the comparisons. For a super self-torture trip, use an old school chum who became

> Supreme Court Justice
> congresswoman
> best-selling author
> millionaire in real estate.

Notice that when you refuse to make mental comparisons between yourself and other people, this self-torture game comes to a screeching halt!

8. *The Blame Game.*
If you would only change _____, we could _____. It is all *your* fault that my life is ruined.

9. *Lamenting the Hole in the Doughnut.*
I wish she would do _____ and _____ for me (while quite ignoring all the things she DOES do for you).

10. *The Gloom-and-Doom Pessimism Trip.*
What's the use of trying? _____ and _____ will happen no matter *what* I do.

11. *The Neighbors-Are-Watching Trip.*
What will people think if

> I divorce my wife?
> my kid gets busted?
> I stay with my wife?
> I have an affair?
> I declare bankruptcy?
> And so on.

12. *The Sentimental Memory Game.*

This game is typically done best by middle-aged and elderly couples; however, some younger people have proved to be remarkably proficient at it, also.

Wasn't it wonderful when

> the children were little
> we had no children
> we lived in Baltimore
> Mother was alive
> we were in the Peace Corps
> And so on.

13. *The I'm-Not-Living-Up-to-My-Potential Trip.*

I'm only doing _____ and I could be doing _____.

Some common elements in these self-torture trips (and I'll leave it up to you to define the remaining twenty-six) are the negative feelings engendered, the time wasted, and the focus on the past or future instead of the present. If you are feeling unhappy, objectively observe the "source" of your unhappiness. My guess is that you will find that you are entertaining thoughts or fantasies about the future or the past. Fear of the future and regret for the past are the twin clouds that hide the sunshine of present happiness.

Daydream Junkies

A less pernicious example of someone permitting his fantasy life to take over is Walter Mitty in James Thurber's classic short story. In the course of an afternoon's shopping trip to Waterbury with his domineering wife, Walter blanks out and takes on several different roles—brilliant surgeon, expert sharpshooter, heroic military pilot, and the undaunted man about to face a firing squad ("To hell with the handkerchief!")—that bear no resemblance to his actual life with the redoubtable Mrs. Mitty. (He launches himself into his surgeon role, "hastily pulling on his gloves" after a contemptuous admonition from his wife to wear his gloves.) Had Walter asked himself the two magic questions, he might well have realized, "I'm daydreaming. I'm casting myself in a heroic role that is quite different from the way my wife sees me." Possibly he would have taken a look at his actual life and seen how bitterly unsatisfying it was . . . and then have taken some action to change.

People who indulge excessively and without awareness in the Walter Mitty-type of fantasies are daydream junkies. They use these fantasies to compensate for the dreariness of their actual lives. If they would examine their daydreams, they would learn how they want their lives to be, and could then constructively plan for these changes. This is called "grounding," and is an essential part of any fantasy work. Otherwise you could substitute fantasies for actions, become a daydream junkie, and soon require a daily "fix" of idle daydreams.

L'esprit de l'escalier

Do you ever observe yourself, after an event, going back over all the details of the interaction, reconstructing the dialogue, and possibly realizing all the clever things you *could* have said or done? The French call this *l'esprit de l'escalier*, the wit of the staircase. It's the substitution—as you climb the staircase to go to bed after a party—of your now droll and perceptive observations for the dull or, worse yet, clumsy remarks you did make.

This can be a very destructive use of your time if you allow your "critic" subpersonality to be condemning and send you on an If-Only-I-Had self-torture trip. An expert self-torturer can do a jack story here by recalling an inept remark, then imagining "everyone" heard it and thinks badly of him as a result. He can now script the end of his business career or his social life as "everyone" will now boycott his business or forget to invite him to their parties.

The time can be usually well spent, however, if you will reconstruct the event and examine it in a nonjudgmental way. You might notice a more tactful way you could have phrased an opinion or invented a clever *bon mot*. If you will approach such an Evening Review as a learning situation, you can prepare yourself to handle a similar event in the future in a different manner.

This is a very useful exercise to do every evening before you go to sleep:

Evening Review

Have your eyes closed, sit with your spine straight. Take a few deep breaths, observing the circuit of your breathing to help you feel centered. Then review your day, starting with the last minutes before sitting down to do your Evening Review. Go backwards, viewing all the events and activities of the day until the moment of your awakening in the morning and, perhaps, the memory of dreams. Do this without emotion and without judgment. *Review the day, don't relive it.* Recall what you said and what you thought. Don't allow yourself to get into an *If-Only-I-Had* trip. If you have difficulty maintaining detachment when you do this, pretend you are observing the life of another person and love him the way he is.

The purpose of the Evening Review is two-fold: first, to deliberately avoid slipping unconsciously into *l'esprit de l'escalier*, and second, to enlarge your knowledge of yourself and your actions and to develop a greater love and tolerance for them. After you are in the habit of asking yourself the two magic questions frequently throughout the day and become skilled in the art of self-observation, you will find that the Evening Review can be accomplished very quickly: "Oh, yes, there was this, and then there was that, and so on."

Head Chatter

Many people are unaware of just how much time they spend in their heads or of the thoughts they are entertaining. Yet probably most of their energy is devoted to their head chatter: thinking, planning, fantasizing, anticipating, remembering, judging, speculating. Do you know people who seem to "go off into space" and, when you ask them what they were thinking, are unable to tell you? Does this perhaps apply to you?

Let's do an exercise to identify the content of your head chatter NOW.

Putting Labels on Your Thoughts

Find a quiet place where you can sit comfortably with your back straight, without interruption. Have paper and pen with you. Close your eyes. Concentrate on your breathing, first inflating your belly, then allowing air to raise your rib cage and then push into the spaces under your collarbones. Next exhale all your air slowly and completely, making a soft *s-s-s-s* sound as you do it so that you will know when all your air is gone.

Let your new breath come in easily when it wants to, without grabbing for it. Watch the rhythm of your breathing . . . the air coming in, the air going out to the accompaniment of the soft *s-s-s-s* sound. Notice any thought that occurs. Label it, open your eyes to write it down (as briefly as possible). Then dismiss the thought, close your eyes, and resume your concentration on your breathing until the next thought or awareness pops in. And so on. Don't stay with any one thought. We just want to get "soil samples," not complete ideas, in this experiment. Do this for 30 minutes.

Now look at your list. What percentage of the items were sensory awareness (the shaft of light coming in the window, the telephone ringing, cooking smells, the neighbor's sprinkler); what percentage were body awareness (noticing your chest rise more readily after several deliberate breaths, feet feeling cold); and what percentage were thoughts? Examine those thoughts that strayed in.

See how many are planning thoughts—things you want to or "need to" do.

How many are anxiety-provoking thoughts?

Are any of your thoughts out-and-out fantasies of nonexistent but desirable situations? or relationships? or events?

Are some of them envious comparisons? or invidious comparisons?

And most important: Did any of your thoughts seem to "take over," so that you spent a lot of time elaborating on a theme instead of labeling, recording, and clearing your mind according to the instructions for the exercise?

If this happened, you can be sure that this area has a lot of power over you. The time you spend in your head can be used either constructively or destructively. You're in charge of how you use it. But before you can make a responsible choice, you need to learn to be aware of WHAT you are thinking.

It's a good idea to keep tuning into your mind to see what you're thinking. You can visualize a part of yourself as an Objective Observer who is perched on your left shoulder and who will ask frequently, "OK, what are you thinking about RIGHT NOW?" Aldous Huxley's *Island* was populated with mynah birds that were trained to say "Attention" and "Here and now, boys." The philosophy of everyday living in this utopian kingdom was based on awareness, so the function of the birds was to remind people to pay attention to what was happening.

You probably don't have a mynah bird or a parrot to train to be your "come to awareness" reminder, but you can select other staple items of your daily life to use as cues. Whenever you hear a clock strike the hour, you could ask yourself,

What am I thinking, feeling, doing, RIGHT NOW?

What do I want for myself RIGHT NOW?

Someone I know has trained herself to ask the two magic questions every time she goes through a doorway. Since she keeps house, she spends her day passing back and forth through many doorways, doing tasks that could lead to mental and emotional numbness unless she makes an effort to stay aware.

You could use the telephone as a device to trigger the use of the two magic questions. When the phone rings, ask yourself how you feel about the interruption. Check into your fantasies about who is calling. If you're not aware that you're hoping that George will be on the other end of the line, you may not be prepared for the subtle hostility you feel when it turns out to be John, instead of George.

If you center yourself by checking in on your thoughts and feelings before making a phone call, you will be better informed about what you really want and in a better place to handle the interaction successfully.

Ideally, we can be completely aware of the present (or "mindful," as the Buddhists call it) every second of every minute. Thich Nhat Hanh in a delightful book, *The Miracle of Mindfulness*, illustrates this with the homely occupation of dishwashing:

> If while washing dishes, we think only of the cup of tea that awaits us, thus hurrying to get the dishes out of the way as if they were a nuisance, . . . we are not alive during the time we are washing the dishes. In fact, we are completely incapable of realizing the miracle of life while standing at the sink. If we can't wash the dishes [with awareness], the chances are we won't be able to drink our tea [with awareness] either. While drinking the cup of tea, we will only be thinking of other things, barely aware of the cup in our hands. Thus we are sucked away into the future—and we are incapable of actually living one minute of life.

What is your reaction to this quotation? How do you typically wash the dishes?

Subpersonalities

For many people their minds seem to be battlegrounds where different strident voices struggle for supremacy. One might be saying:

> Ann, you've got to study tonight. You want to make a good grade in this course, so you can get into medical school, so you can have a meaningful career . . .

Another voice might counter:

> Good grief, another night of studying? How long has it been since you've had any fun, Ann? Why don't you call Charlie and see if he wants to go to a movie or something or just go to bed, maybe?

And a third would chide:

> You don't want to see Charlie. You're still grieving for Sam. You turned him off by all this dedication to school and career. Are you sure you wouldn't rather be a housewife and mother like Mom?

And the voice goes on to evoke all the desirable and beloved qualities of the departed Sam.

A number of different psychologists in constructing their theories of personality have taken into account these differing aspects of the personality. Sigmund Freud would have identified the first voice as "superego" and the second as "id." Fritz Perls would have called them "Topdog" and "Underdog," whereas Eric Berne would call them "Parent" and "Child."

These systems can be very useful, but a disadvantage is that the elements can be defined by the therapists within each of the systems in such a way as to emphasize the universal qualities of each element and to downplay the individualistic and idiosyncratic qualities in each person. For instance, Fritz Perls says, "The topdog is a bully [who] manipulates with demands and threats of catastrophe . . . The underdog manipulates with being defensive, apologetic, wheedling, playing the cry-baby, and such."

In the system of Roberto Assagioli, however, each of the three voices would be considered to be subpersonalities and Ann would be asked to name them herself. She gave them these names: Ambitious Annie, The Playgirl, and The Lonely Heart. As she has learned by working with her subpersonalities, Ambitious Annie is that part of her that wants to be "successful," that doesn't want to be trapped in a life of borderline poverty like her parents, that felt nourished and encouraged by her teachers who saw her as especially bright and competent.

The Playgirl is that part of her that wants to have fun, that resents Ambitious Annie's two jobs and pursuit of top grades that deny her the pleasures her friends have. The Lonely Heart is that part of her that recognizes the enviable attributes of her parents' life and wants them for herself, too.

Every subpersonality is organized around a "want" of the total personality. The strength of each want and of the resultant subpersonality is probably attributable to the circumstances in which the want was initially born. I prefer not to use the labels of Topdog, Underdog, Parent, Child, and so on. I would rather have someone examine, identify, and get to know the voices in his own head and to give each voice its own individual name. One of these subpersonalities will undoubtedly be a species of the genus Topdog. However, my Prosecuting Attorney is different from your Spiteful Demon, who is different from his Critic or Ann's Ambitious Annie.

The range of subpersonalities within each person is vast. There is a subpersonality for each role we play in the world: the Parent, the Child, the Boss, the Employee, the Professor, the Student, the Healer, the Patient, the Consumer, the Entrepreneur, and so on. (Most of us have minor subpersonalities with differing attitudes toward traffic problems: the Pedestrian and the Automobile Driver. Is this true for you, or have you been able to synthesize these two role subpersonalities?)

Each person has a rich mix of highly individual subpersonalities that, when fully examined, are identical with no other person's group of subpersonalities.

But instead of talking about it, let's do this exercise for identifying some of your subpersonalities:

---

*The Doughnut**

1. Make a list of all your wants. Write quickly and include everything that comes to your mind. Material things as well as nonmaterial things. Be sure you have included those items that you currently enjoy and want to continue having. This isn't a what-I-want-for-Christmas list!
Since you may be doing this alone and, therefore, without access to other peoples' lists, I want to mention some high-frequency wants that others have:

> to be healthy
> to be a good parent
> to make a lot of money
> to finish schooling
> to succeed in business/profession
> to be a loving partner to someone
> to be loved by others
> to become enlightened

---

*This is a modification of Tom Yeomans' Pie exercise.

2. Now, keep aware of what you're feeling as you read this list I gave you. Is there a subpersonality telling you that you should have all those wants, too? Or criticizing people who have certain wants that either you don't have or would place at a low priority? Make a list of your *own* wants.

3. When your list reaches 20 items (or whenever you feel you have listed *every* want), examine your list and select the five or six most important wants. You may want to rewrite some of your items. For example, you could telescope "skiing," "swimming," "backpacking," and "tennis," into "doing sports and being outdoors." Again, give priority to *your* most important wants, and don't include those that your What-Will-People-Think subpersonality wants to give a higher billing.

4. Now, on a large piece of drawing paper draw a doughnut that is 12 inches to 18 inches in diameter. Consider the center portion to represent your Self. In the doughnut we will house the five or six subpersonalities that are expressed in these wants.

5. Now draw symbols (using oil pastels or any other color medium) to represent each of your wants. Don't worry about your artistic ability or alleged lack of it. Just quickly draw and color whatever symbols emerge for you.

6. When you have finished your drawing, find a name for each of the subpersonalities. Some of your names for them may seem like stock names: the Adventurer, the Good Provider, Needed Nellie, the Healthy One, the Healer, Earth Mother, the Lover, the Contented Knower. Other subpersonalities may emerge with very idiosyncratic and descriptive names such as Primitive Tender of Horse and Hound, Peripatetic Gemini Jan (this one of mine represents the restless, adventurous part of me that wants to travel and explore new things), Farm Girl alias Wood Elf, Atlas, Ms. God, Ben Casey, and so on. It's important for you to derive your own set of names that will have meaning for you.

7. Now color your Self however you wish.

This is an exercise you can repeat many times. I think you will find that certain subpersonalities consistently make the "top five" list, and their names may change as you come to know more clearly what they want, how they operate, and how they change over time.

The games that your subpersonalities play in your head can be destructive when you are not aware of them or when you allow yourself to become stalemated and immobilized by their conflict. One of the goals in self-observation is to become ever more aware of the central self and give it the power to arbitrate among the warring subpersonalities. It won't work to try to ignore or banish any of the subpersonalities because each is organized around a legitimate want of the total personality.

Ann had a labor/management negotiation conference with her three subpersonalities. Playgirl settled for having fun one night a week, with the stipulation that Ambitious Annie was to make *no* remarks about unread books or unwritten papers for that evening. Lonely Heart admitted that she had been doing a Sentimental Memory self-torture trip. She conceded that it would not have worked out with Sam, because that would have meant the death of Ambitious Annie, so Lonely Heart agreed to stop playing "poor me" about the end of that relationship.

Ambitious Annie promised to modify her demands the next time a likely candidate for future husband came along.

Here is an exercise in which you can learn more about some of your subpersonalities:

Doughnut Dialogue

Have each of the identified subpersonalities in the dough-nut converse with every other subpersonality and with the Self. Have them say what they appreciate about one another, what they resent, and what each wants from the other. You may want to write these dialogues in your journal or a notebook if you are doing these exercises alone. In that case I would recommend that you do only a few dialogues at one sitting, but take the time to develop each interaction fully. (Five subpersonalities and the Self = fifteen dialogues. Six subpersonalities and the Self = twenty-one dialogues.) Have them say sentences to another that begin with:

"I like . . ."
"I resent . . ."
"I want you to . . ."
"I imagine that you . . ."

The following is an exercise you can do in a group that will audibly demonstrate the clashing of the subpersonalities' voices in your head:

Subpersonality Psychodrama

Pick someone to play each of your subpersonalities. (Give them a few lines of sample dialogue so that they will be able to play *your* subpersonalities and not theirs!)

Sit in the center of the room and have your actor-friends sitting close around you.

On signal they should all start talking to you at once—wheedling, cajoling, demanding, threatening. Stay in touch with your Self, notice how you feel about the statements and actions of each.

Be in control. Like an orchestra conductor, put up your hands to silence (or tone down) an overly-strident sub-personality, or to encourage and amplify a timid one.

When you've had it, yell "uncle" for them to stop. Now tell each of your subpersonalities how you felt about what they said and did, and the importance you intend to give each of them in your life in the future.

End by thanking each of your friends and dismissing them from their roles.

For some people this is a most revealing exercise. "This is just what it sounds like in my head all the time!" Some begin to realize the power of the Self, and that they can modulate the voices and demands of a subpersonality in real life, even more than they can in this psychodrama situation.

Topdogs and Critics

The Doughnut exercise probably revealed subpersonalities whose surface qualities are positive (even though they may have been in conflict with one another). Most of us have several subpersonalities whose surface qualities are negative. One is the Critic subpersonality, or Topdog. Here is an exercise to help you define it more precisely:

Defining Your Critic

What does it say to you?
Possibly sentences starting with "You should . . ." and "When will you ever learn to . . ."
        In what tone of voice?
        When does it appear?
        What things does it do?
        How do you feel about
            this subpersonality?

Give it a name that will express its essence. If you think of a noun, then supply an adjective or two to describe its attributes even more specifically.

Some names others have chosen: the Persecutor, the District Attorney, Put-Her-Down, Cut-Her-Down-To-Size Critic, the Subtle Underminer, "You're a dummy . . . there you go again." And also: Slasher, Ms. Perfect, Reproacher, Pusher, and Global Killer. What have you named *your* Critic?

Now be the Critic subpersonality. Tell the total personality how much it needs you. Describe what a mess it would be in without you.

As your Self, acknowledge the valuable side of the Critic subpersonality. Negotiate with him about how you can retain and use the positive parts, and tone down the abrasive and negative parts. The flip side of a Persecutor may be a Protector or an Instigator.

Saboteurs and Victims

Another negative-appearing subpersonality is the genus Saboteur. He surfaces sometimes when you least expect him. He may discourage you from undertaking some new venture, or wreck one that's already under way. Identifying and understanding your saboteur can be some of the most important work you do on yourself.

Meet Your Saboteur

1. Visualize a project that you want to do and do successfully. It might be having twenty people for dinner on Thanksgiving, raising a family, finishing school, or starting a healing center. See your project in existence and flourishing.

2. Now, what could happen to damage your project, to sabotage it? Visualize this.

3. Draw a picture of the saboteur or the sabotaging force.

4. Now *be* the saboteur and deliberately sabotage the project. Tell what is the payoff for you in having the project fail.

5. Now from the perspective of the Self, confront the saboteur. Negotiate with him.

Brent was an artist, and a good artist. He dreamed of giving up his regular and rather unsatisfying job so he could paint full time. He saved enough money to give himself a cushion for a year of economical living and was on the verge of giving notice when his Saboteur scared him out of it: "Suppose you don't succeed? Suppose you don't sell enough this year to live on next year? You probably won't be able to get your job back or any other job that pays this well or with as good security. Everyone says there's a big depression coming, and you'd better not do anything crazy." He recognized the voice as that of his mother, who had enjoyed predicting disaster and telling his father, "I told you so." Brent felt Cassandra would be an apt name for his saboteur subpersonality. Other saboteurs have been named:

Sweet Bitch	Time Bandit
The Paranoid	The Destroyer
The Devil	The Nag
Rebellious Child	Sharon Should and Shall
Why-Try?-Everything- Is-Useless	Worry Bomb The Fault Finder
If You Can't Be the Best, Give Up	The Vengeful Killer

One person called his saboteur the Two-edged Sword. One blade he called the Exhorting Record-Setter, who rushed him with "time is of the essence"; the other blade was called Time-is-Eternal, and soothed, "Don't rush, don't hassle."

Another bipolar saboteur who can freeze you into anxious immobility is the one who says alternately, "Nothing ventured, nothing gained, *do* it," and "Be careful, don't be hasty."

What have you named *your* saboteur subpersonality?

Possibly your saboteur is also your Victim subpersonality, which is a subpersonality that most of us have and can discover. It's that part of you that enjoys being a victim, being helpless, getting attention by virtue of being inadequate, and so on. Some Victim subpersonalities that I have met have been named:

Iceberg of Fear
Angry, Neglected Child
The Spiteful Hermit
The Empty Cup
Selfish, Sassy Person
Helpless Procrastinator
Mom
Multi-directed Oyster
n0thing

A Victim subpersonality can have its genesis in a childhood situation where the person was truly victimized. One young woman had been born to a mother who didn't want her, yet wouldn't release her for adoption either. So Wanda was passed from relative to relative to foster home, living no more than a year or two in any place and always feeling (possibly realistically) unwanted. She is now grown and happily married to a husband who *does* want her, yet she has a Waif Wanda subpersonality who feels that she doesn't belong. As a child she had to straddle the conflicting values of her last home and her current home, desperately trying to think and behave according to the standards of the new home and fearing disapproval when she unthinkingly echoed the beliefs of the old home. Similarly today Waif Wanda becomes anxious and upset when members of her husband's family disagree on politics or religion or morality.

Obsolete Behavior Patterns

Someone who was a genuine Victim as a child can learn patterns of behavior (and accompanying feelings) that persist long after the need for such behavior has passed.

Frances was the victim of a molesting stepfather. From having her play with his genitals when she was five, he progressed to full sexual intercourse at age twelve, all the while warning her not to tell her mother because her mother would then be angry, throw her out of the house, and not love her any more. Frances, like most child victims of a molesting male, felt helpless to change her circumstances or to do anything but go along with her stepfather's demands.* Now her Victim subpersonality frequently feels she has to comply in other unpleasant situations and persists in feeling that she has no power to change events. This includes situations where she is obviously in charge, such as making an appointment for a haircut or "going on a diet." Her Victim is taking her on a "What's the use? I can't change anything" self-torture trip and is also sabotaging her from taking responsibility for her life.

---

* If this case sounds unusual to you, let me give you the estimate of San Francisco's Sexual Trauma Center: One out of every four children in the United States is sexually abused or used by age fifteen. Also not unusual is the shame that they frequently feel. Frances, for instance, started therapy to deal with these feelings of shame. She hesitated through several sessions before she felt free to tell me her story. Afterwards she showed me a tattered professional card of mine that she had been carrying in her wallet for eighteen months while trying to summon the courage to call me. She had been afraid that when I heard her story I would be so disgusted that I would throw her out of my office and refuse to see her again. (I'm including this anecdote at Frances' specific request for the benefit of other women who have had similar experiences and may feel they are unique.)

One thing that these subpersonalities—Cassandra, Waif Wanda, and What's-the-Use?—have in common is their preoccupation with past and future and their refusal to accept the reality of Now. Frances, like Brent and Wanda, had to come to terms with her past, had to grieve with the afflicted child-that-she-was, and then could tell her Victim subpersonality quite firmly, "Things are different now."

It's important not to condemn yourself for having negative-appearing subpersonalities. The flip side will always reveal the positive, life-sustaining features. Waif Wanda is sensitive to the needs of a stranger in her home and is an excellent hostess. Cassandra will always be available to keep Brent from overdrawing his checking account. Acceptance—*owning*—of your "negative" subpersonalities, traits, motives, actions is the key to growth and happiness. This doesn't mean identifying with them or allowing your Self to be controlled by them, however.

This is a good place to introduce the concept of disidentification, which is an important and ancient practice. The following exercise is adapted from Assagioli's *Psychosynthesis*.

Disidentification Exercise

Sit comfortably with your spine erect. Close your eyes. Take a few deep breaths while mentally following the circuit of your breath. Then affirm the following, either aloud or silently:

I *have* a body, but *I am not* my body.
My body may be sick or well, tired or rested, but that has nothing to do with my Self, my real "I".
My body is my precious instrument of experience and of action in the outer world, but it is *only* an instrument. I treat it well; I seek to keep it in good health, but it is *not* my self.
I *have* a body, but *I am not* my body.

I *have* emotions, but *I am not* my emotions.
My emotions are many, contradictory, and changing.
Yet I always remain I, *my self*, whether in joy or in pain, whether calm or annoyed, whether hopeful or despairing. Since I can observe, understand and label my emotions, and then increasingly dominate, direct and utilize them, it is evident that they are not *myself*.
I *have* emotions, but *I am not* my emotions.

I *have* an intellect but *I am not* my intellect.
It is more or less developed and active.
It is my tool for knowing both the outer world and my inner world, but *it is not myself*.
I *have* an intellect, but *I am not* my intellect.

I *am* a center of pure self-consciousness.
I *am* a Center of Will, capable of mastering and directing my intellect, my physical body, my emotions, and all my psychological processes.
I *am* the constant and unchanging Self.

This is a valuable exercise to do over and over again. It ultimately becomes an exercise in *self*-identification, because as you learn to disidentify from your feelings, body, mind, thoughts, and subpersonalities, you get more into the experience of the real "I," which is simple, constant, unchanging, immutable.

You can use this disidentification model with any of your subpersonalities, writing your own descriptive sentences, and ending with the disidentifying "I *have* a Waif Wanda subpersonality, but *I am not* Waif Wanda."

You're In Charge of Your Visualizations
You are in charge of the images that you create in your mind. Let's demonstrate:

Visualization Demonstration Exercise

You can lie down for this one if you like.

Close your eyes. Concentrate on your breathing for a few circuits.

Now visualize a large blank white movie screen.

Now visualize a flower on the screen, any kind of flower. Now take this flower off the screen; replace it with a white rose.

Now change this white rose to a red one. (If you have difficulty doing this, imagine yourself with a paint brush painting the rose red, as in *Alice in Wonderland*.)

Now take away the rose and visualize the room you are in: its furniture, the colors, textures, arrangement, and so on.

Now turn the picture upside down. See the furniture suspended from the ceiling. (If this is hard, imagine yourself up on the ceiling looking down on the room and its contents.)

Now visualize a large blank white movie screen again.

Now put a blue filter in front of the light so that the whole screen becomes bright blue.

Now change the filter to red.

Now make the screen green.

Now create some color and design of your own choosing.

If this is the first time you have tried an exercise like this, you may not have been able to produce all the effects, such as turning the room upside down or changing the colors. These are easier to do when you are lying down, relaxed, and someone is reading you the suggestions. I imagine, however, that you successfully saw the blank screen, produced a flower, and visualized your current surroundings with your eyes closed. This should be sufficient "proof" that you are responsible for the images that you produce. So if you ever find yourself looking at a mental image that causes you distress, realize that you are responsible for it, that you created it, and that you can substitute a new and more pleasant image just as you painted the *white* rose *red*.

I'm now going to give you a number of fantasy exercises that can be constructive uses of your fantasy time. It's useful to have a relaxation prelude with some or all of the following suggestions before launching into the fantasy itself.

Relaxation Prelude

Find a comfortable position in which your spine is straight.

Close your eyes.

Concentrate on your breathing. Let your breath first fill your belly and then inflate your chest, spreading into the two horns of your lungs that extend up under your collarbones.

Let your breath leave as easily as it entered. Make a small, soft sigh as you exhale. Make sure you breathe all of your air out.

Then let the new breath enter as it needs to, without rushing or forcing.

Notice what parts of your body are in contact with chair, floor, bed, or ground. At each place the surface is supporting you, let yourself give over a little bit more to that support. Imagine the chair/floor/bed/ground rising up to hold you. Relax any muscles you have been using to hold yourself up.

An exercise for when you are feeling hassled, or for when you feel you need to be in control, and are afraid of being "out of control":

The Cork on the Ocean

Imagine that you are a little cork in the middle of a large ocean . . . You have no direction, no goal, no compass, no rudder, no oars . . . You drift wherever the wind and the ocean currents send you . . . A big wave may come along and submerge you temporarily, but you bob right back up to the surface again . . . Allow yourself to experience this drifting and bobbing on the surface of the ocean . . . Experience the push of the waves . . . the warmth of the sun . . . the staccato of the rain . . . the cushion of the sea beneath you, supporting you . . . See what other experiences you create as a little cork in the middle of a big ocean.

The "as-if" exercise:

If you are feeling depressed, imagine how you would feel and all the things you would do if you were not depressed.

If you are feeling powerless, imagine what you would be like if you were powerful.

If you are feeling tired, get in touch with that part of you that never tires. Imagine yourself fully energized. What do you do? How do you feel?

When you need some psychic recharging:

Reliving Past Positives

1. Think back over your life for those times when you knew you were truly loved. Pick one and re-live it in all its detail.

or

Think back over your life for those peak experiences . . . those times when you were in love . . . or were listening to music . . . or got some oceanic insight . . . or were caught up in creating something . . . or were immersed in a book or some activity. Pick one of these peak experiences and relive it.

2. Now ask yourself, what are the essential qualities of that experience?

3. And how are you keeping yourself from feeling that way *Now*?

I have a favorite peak experience to which I have returned many times, each time feeling at least a faint echo of the tremendous charge of the original experience. Back in the days when I was a wife and mother, I used to go sit in the cockpit of our small sloop moored off Coconut Grove, Florida. And write or think about writing. One day I allowed myself to be caught up in the experience of *Now*—the stillness, the water, the sun, the clouds—and was filled with the most ineffable love for it all, for everything, for everybody. The wish that sprang into my mind was, "World, let me embrace you." This probably doesn't say much to you; peak experiences seem not easily communicated through words. I share it only as an example; the important thing is for you to honor your *own* peak experiences.

After you do the following fantasy exercise, you will know which times in your life it will be a useful exercise for you:

Temple of Silence

Imagine that you are walking on the sidewalk of a crowded and noisy city . . . Feel your feet on the pavement . . . Notice the other pedestrians as you pass them, their faces, their expressions, their bodies . . . Notice that some seem rushed, while others seem relaxed and joyful. Notice the traffic, its speed, its noise . . . the horns honking, the brakes squealing . . . Any other noises? . . . Notice the windows of the shops as you pass their displays . . . a hardware store, a florist shop . . . Perhaps you see a familiar face in the crowd. Do you stop and greet this person? Or do you pass on? Stay in touch with how you are feeling on this busy, noisy street. Now turn the corner and go down a less hectic side street. As you go down the street you notice a large building whose architecture doesn't fit with the other buildings. The large clear sign over the door reads "The Temple of Silence." You realize the temple is a place where no sounds are made, where no words have ever been uttered . . . You reach up and touch the heavy, carved wooden doors. You push one open and enter and are immediately surrounded with complete and total silence . . . .
. . . .

When you are ready to leave the building, push open the wooden doors, go back out into the city, and see how you feel now. Remember the way to the side street so that you can make a return visit to the Temple of Silence whenever you wish.

After any of these fantasy exercises it is useful to record your experience in your bound notebook. What did you learn from doing the exercise? Anything that you can use in your non-fantasy life? Remember that relating your fantasy to your life in the outer world is called "grounding," and will save you from becoming a daydream junkie.

Here is an exercise to use when your energy level is low:

Energy Induction

Imagine a source of energy in front of you. See it warming you, energizing you. Feel the energy surging through the whole front of you.

Breathe it in with your incoming breath. Now visualize this same symbol or source of energy behind you. Feel the energy coursing up and down your back.

Now picture the energy on your right side. Feel your whole right side being energized.

Now place the energy source at your left side. Feel the whole left side of your body being energized.

Now imagine the energy source above you. Feel the top of your head being energized.

Now place the energy source below you. Feel the soles of your feet being energized, and now the energy is rising, permeating your entire body.

Now imagine yourself sending energy out to some other person; now send energy to a second person. Be aware of which people you select. Now send your energy to your family and to your various groups and communities.

Here's an exercise for those times when you feel overwhelmed with many tasks to do and lack guidelines about which to tackle first:

The Secret Garden

You're taking a walk on the grounds of a large estate. You see a high stone wall that is practically obscured with ivy. In the wall you notice a wooden door. On impulse you push open the wooden door and step through. You realize that you are inside an old walled garden. It's a garden that must once have been a lovely, formal garden, but no one has been tending it. The plants are so overgrown and there are so many weeds that it's hard to tell which are paths and which are garden plots. Starting with one part of the garden, see yourself pruning, weeding, mowing, cultivating, transplanting, watering and doing whatever needs to be done to put the garden back in order again . . . If you need any encouragement, stand back and compare the part of the garden you have been working on with the part that you haven't touched.

The following exercise is a good one for those occasions when you are feeling insecure, vulnerable, or "deserted."

The Lighthouse

Visualize a small rocky island off the coast of a continent. On the highest spot of the island is a tall, solidly constructed lighthouse. Imagine yourself as that lighthouse, with your base firmly anchored in the rock of the island. Your walls are thick and sturdy so that, despite your height, you do not bend or sway in the high winds that frequently blow across this island. From the windows in your top you send out a steady sweep of light, by day and by night, in good weather and bad. Be aware of all the auxiliary power systems you have that ensure the constancy of your light beam sweeping its circular path across the ocean, warning the ships of the shoals, offering a symbol of security to the people on the shore.

Now feel that center of inner light within you, that light that can never be extinguished.

Now as we're ending Chapter 2, let's do a little self-observation. What are you aware of *right now*? Recapitulate the various things you have noticed and learned about yourself from the various exercises in this chapter. And observe, *right now*, your reaction to these last suggestions!

The art of self-observation is a major method for learning how to take charge of our thoughts, feelings, and emotions. It's very important that in the beginning of self-observation we simply observe ourselves as we are without analyzing, condemning, or attempting to change ourselves. We are compiling an album of "mental photographs" of ourselves, taken by a neutral camera at different moments of different situations and of varying emotional states. "Here's one of me crying, here's one of me feeling triumphant, here's one of me being confused," and so on.

Make these observations, take these mental photographs without judgment or condemnation or attempts to improve yourself. Otherwise you are off on an introspective self-torture trip. If you want to understand, you must *observe*. Not criticize. Not judge. When you are trying to improve yourself, you of necessity have to make judgments. As long as you are making judgments, you will not allow yourself to self-observe, to see yourself just as you are.

Chapters Four, Five, Six, and Seven are devoted to specific tools that will be helpful in learning the art of self-observation. They will deal with journals, autobiographies, dreams, and meditation. But first let's examine our relationships with Important Other People.

CHAPTER 3

YOU'RE IN CHARGE OF YOUR INTERPERSONAL RELATIONSHIPS: GETTING ALONG WITH OTHER PEOPLE

If you feel you are having problems in your relationship with another, perhaps the real problem lies in important issues within yourself that you have not yet observed. Possibly in one or more of the following areas:

Expectations
"Security"
Control
Need for affection and approval
Moral indignation (which will turn out
    to be a variation of Expections)
Unfinished business with another Other

Or there may be a subpersonality preventing you from relating to Others in the healthiest possible manner—your Victim or your Saboteur, perhaps.

Before we examine each of these areas, let's do an exercise to see where you are with an important person in your life.

Significant Other Exercise

Sit comfortably.

Close your eyes.

Choose a Significant Other for the purposes of this exercise. It could be a spouse, a lover, a co-worker, a sibling . . . It should be someone who is important to you at this moment (regardless whether the person is living or dead).

Who was the first person you thought of? . . . If you are not using that person in the exercise, be clear with yourself why not.

Place the Significant Other in front of you . . . Visualize his posture, clothing, activity, expression.

Now talk to this person. Tell him what you appreciate about him. Don't stop at one or two items; search your mind and heart for a full list.

Now tell him what you resent about him. Again, don't stop with one or two items. Name every resentment, especially those you have resisted telling him . . .

Now tell him what you expect of him, what you want from him.

Now imagine that five years have passed. Tell him how you imagine your relationship will be then . . . how you will feel about each other, what your situation will be. (You can also tell him how you *hope* it will be.)

I think you will find this exercise is a useful one to clarify how you are currently feeling about a Significant Other. If you are having difficulties with this person, it can be helpful to write out the exercise, or to talk it into a tape recorder, or—best of all—to say it to the person directly and have him do the same exercise with you.

Expectations

> Each man is his own absolute law-giver, the dispenser of glory or gloom to himself; the decreer of his life, his reward, his punishment.
> —Mabel Collins in *The Idyll of the White Lotus*

A great many people come to therapy because they "have been so hurt" by other people. I'm sure we all have known many such people. There was Ruth, whose manfriend was spending less and less time with her. She called him to ask him to come over; he declined, and she was very hurt. Kathleen is an older woman who became very hurt when her eighty-year-old mother could not find time to see her or call her but seemed to have plenty of time for Kathleen's sister. Dan was hurt each time that his wife failed to come to bed at his bedtime; he bore a continuing hurt that she didn't seem to regret their resulting sexual infrequency. Some other people in identical situations would label their emotional reaction "anger" and wonder about the "hurt" that Ruth, Kathleen, and Dan felt. I believe that there is hurt underlying their anger. People who are unwilling to experience the pain of being hurt may direct their emotional indicators to spin quickly from "hurt" to "anger" to spare themselves. (Conversely, those people who are afraid to deal with their own angry feelings don't allow their emotions to move from "hurt" to "anger," but persist in feeling hurt.)

Regardless of the emotion experienced, the cause is the same: expectations. Ruth, unrealistically ignoring her manfriend's new behavior pattern, *expected* that he would be willing to come over when she invited him and therefore was dashed, disappointed, and hurt when he refused. Kathleen, despite a good forty years of being ignored by her mother in preference to the favored sister, persisted in *expecting* that her mother would respond to her overtures. When her mother turned her down, she was first hurt and then angry. And Dan, because he loved and desired his wife, imagined that she had a reciprocal feeling and so he *expected* that she would want to go to bed and make love.

I'm happy to report that all three of these people learned the art of self-observation and began to recognize that they were setting themselves up for hurt and anger by expecting certain behaviors from their Significant Others. When they were willing to let go of their wishes and expectations, they were no longer "hurt" by their Others.

Notice the kinds of expectations you have of others. Do you expect your spouse or lover to be sexually faithful? To always want to do what you want to do? To love you forever? To take out the garbage? To always remember your birthday?

To "make you happy"? You put an impossible burden on a relationship when you expect the other person to make you happy or when you hold her responsible for your happiness. One of the most valuable things you can learn from the art of self-observation is how you "happy" and "unhappy" yourself by the thoughts and fantasies that you hold.

Let's play a game. Let's pretend that happiness is humanity's natural state and that your Happiness Quotient is a constant 100—except for those times that you bring yourself down by any of the 39 self-torture trips.

Happiness Quotient Exercise

Sit comfortably.

Take a few Complete Breaths.

What is your Happiness Quotient right now? Your normal 100?

If so, congratulations!

If not, observe yourself until you can identify what you are doing to prevent yourself from enjoying a normal HQ.

Are you worrying about the possible future?

Are you worrying about the past and doing *l'esprit de l'escalier*?

Are you comparing yourself to someone else?

Are you feeling unjustly treated by someone?

Are you plotting revenge?

Are you feeling "What's the use, everything is hopeless"?

If you answered "yes" to any of the above, here's an antidote that may bring your HQ back to normal:

Happiness Quotient Exercise II

Make a list of everything you have to be grateful for right now. Be sure to include all the things that you may take for granted: a sunny day, money in the bank (watch it, don't do an ungrateful that the sum is not larger!), your health, health of your family, shelter, food, beauty, love, peace.

You may remember the story of the two individuals who are shown a half glass of water. One says, "It is half full and I am grateful." The other says, "It is half empty and I feel cheated." The difference in the two people is not in what they have, but their attitude about what they have. People who have learned the art of genuine gratitude* are more apt to be emotionally and physically sound, as well as sought-after companions, than are those "cheated" people whose cups are always half empty.

So many people exhaust themselves with the pursuit of happiness. "After I get married, I will be happy." "After my children are grown and educated and happy, I will be happy." I don't believe that happiness is something to be pursued. Rather it seems to be a state of inner freedom, freedom from worries, self-doubts, fears, blind obedience to custom and society, competitive strivings, awe and envy of others. So don't expect another to "make you happy."

Conversely, you take on an impossible task if you expect to make your Other happy. It's an ego trip to think that you can, that you have that kind of power. It's a control trip to be determined that you will; and it's a self-torture trip to stay in a deadening relationship to prevent the catastrophic unhappiness of the Other if you should do what you want for yourself, which is to get out.

---

*I don't mean the Pollyannas of the world who see everything as wonderful and refuse to perceive the negative facts of their existence.

In all the resentment inventories that I've heard couples throw at one another in parting, this is one of the most bizarre items: Among many other things, Leonard accused Mary—whom he'd lived with for a year—of knowing the secret of happiness and deliberately withholding it from him! What makes this story even sadder is that they were both mental health professionals. Moreover, she took the charge seriously and brooded over it for several weeks, playing "If-Only-I-Had."

"Security"

> You cannot step twice into the same river; for
> fresh waters are ever flowing in upon you.
> —Heraclitus

People who fear the future attempt to "secure" themselves—with money, property, health insurance, personal relationships, marriage contracts. Parents attempt to bind their children to them. Some fearful children are reluctant to leave the home nest. Husbands and wives try to guarantee the continuance of the Other's love and services. This possessiveness and the strictures demanded by the possessive person frequently make the possessed one feel restless and resentful.

The harsh psychological truth is that there is no permanence in human relationships, any more than there is in the stock market, the weather, "national security," and so on. The adoring, somewhat dependent eight-year-old will change into the rebellious, independent teenager (who, if the parents will weather this change, will turn into the responsible and loving adult son or daughter).

Think back to the exercise with your Significant Other. Were you asking him not to change? Were you asking her to return to some earlier (more satisfactory to you) form of behavior? Were you attempting to "secure" his future presence and conduct in any way? This clutching at security can be very damaging to interpersonal relationships, and will impede your own self-growth. The more each of us can learn to be truly in the present with our Others, making no rules and erecting no fences for the future, the stronger we will be in ourselves and the closer and happier in our relationships.

Germaine Greer comments in *The Female Eunuch:*

> Lovers who are free to go when they are restless always come back; lovers who are free to change remain interesting. The bitter animosity and obscenity of divorce is unknown where individuals have not become Siamese twins. A lover who comes to your bed of his own accord is more likely to sleep with his arms around you all night than a lover who has nowhere else to sleep.

She was writing to women, of course. However, the same admonitions may be applied to men in contemporary love relationships. The modern woman will resist emotional chaining, and she will be more fascinating to her man if he permits her inevitable changing. I see many middle-aged husbands who are initially quite panicked by the changes in their wives: the homebody/mother/hostess wants to get a job and have her own world of contacts that are independent of him. He can feel his "security" threatened, that the comforting, habitual pattern of his life is being destroyed, and he may attempt to prohibit or sabotage her efforts to move out into the world. Those men who cooperate with their wives' growth and change are typically rewarded by more interesting companions who bring new dimensions to their husbands' lives.

Some people who have had a very traumatic event in childhood develop a neurotic need for "security." Such a person may then cling to a nonrewarding relationship as "security" so she will not have to undergo a similar ordeal again. What follows is not intended as a check list, but a collection of traumas that happened to real people which might remind you of a childhood trauma of your own:

Esther accidentally swallowed some lye when she was five years old. This was a very painful and frightening experience, as were the several operations she had and the long hospitalizations away from her family and playmates.

Tom, at age eight, had just learned how to get along with kids his own age and had found a gang of boys he felt close to when his family moved to a new city, giving him only a few days' advance notice.

Sarah contracted polio when she was six years old and was put into an isolation ward with no visitors and no phone calls allowed. She was too young to understand the reasons for this isolation; when she cried for her mother, the nurses told her that maybe her mother would come if she would stop crying. When her mother didn't come, they told a variety of lies about "why" the mother couldn't make it. After she was moved to a convalescent ward where her mother could visit her, Sarah would make a scene each time her mother had to leave and would demand that her mother leave a piece of her jewelry as a guarantee of her reappearance.

Tom, now 35, has turned down three promotions that would involve moving to another city, being unwilling to risk losing the "security" of his current relationships. And Sarah is very anxious at the times of her husband's frequent business trips, fearful that he will not return, and insistent that he telephone her every night. Esther lives in a narrow and constricted world, fearful of taking the responsibility for initiating new experiences or making new friends.

The people who attempt to bind their Others to them for fear of not "having" them in the future are in danger of sabotaging their present relationships—to say nothing of their own present enjoyment. For how can I enjoy and appreciate living with you *right now* if I'm spending my time and energy worrying that you may die or leave or no longer love me? Socrates had some good overall advice: "Remember no human condition is ever permanent, then you will not be overjoyed in good fortune, nor too sorrowful in misfortune."

Control

> To love someone is to give
> them room enough to grow.
> —contemporary poster

Those who have not become aware of their fierce needs for "security" are often guilty of trying to control Others in an attempt to block change or control Fate. The mother who decrees what clothing her eight-year-old shall wear (sweater, coat, boots) from fear of his possible cold or pneumonia or death, the husband who finishes his wife's sentences at a party for fear she will jeopardize her good first impression, and the boss who refuses to acknowledge publicly the contributions of his employees for fear they will be hired away from him, are all trying to fix the present and legislate the future. The price is the control (or attempted control) of their Others and the probable ensuing resentment. These control trips are pretty obvious, although possibly not to the perpetrators of them. Some control trips are more devious: the woman who manipulates invitations so that her new manfriend and best womanfriend don't meet, the husband who "forgets" to mention to his alcoholic wife that they are invited to a party where he fears she might drink too much, the mother who manages to shrink her teenage daughter's sweater that she had not liked her to wear because it was "too revealing." Do these examples remind you of any times that you have attempted to control situations or people? If so, recall also the huge amount of energy you had to invest in that effort to control. And what was the final result? What you wanted? Or something else?

Most people report that they feel unhappy when they are trying to control the Other. They can experience anxiety over the imagined terrible things that will happen if the Other doesn't do just what they want. They can also feel angry if they don't get their way. All in all, a control trip is one of the most successful ways to torture yourself.

And how do you feel when you perceive someone as trying to control *you*? What kinds of things do you do and say?

Admittedly, it is rough to be the rejected partner in a dissolving relationship. (Yes, I've been there, too. Haven't we all?) There are many control trips that will occur to the ingenious in an attempt to salvage the situation or to delay the inevitable dissolution. But unless your partner is terribly passive or masochistic, they probably won't work.

There are two final weapons in the Control Trip arsenal that I'd like to warn you about:

1. Illness. You might start thinking, "Gee, if I came down with hepatitis, or broke my leg, or started having convulsions, he wouldn't dare leave me." Energy follows thought, and in the mysterious ways that the mind and body work together, you just might get that illness or infirmity . . . or another. And he might leave anyway. And where would you be then?

2. Threatened suicide. This is the most reprehensible of all control trips: "If you leave, I can't live without you, and I'll kill myself." Anyone who pulls this one deserves to be left. (And anyone who stays with someone who makes such threats deserves to be controlled.)

> Once the realization is accepted that even between the *closest* human beings infinite distances continue to exist, a wonderful living side by side can grow up, if they succeed in loving the distance between them, which makes it possible for each to see the other whole against a wide sky.
>
> —Rainer Maria Rilke

Need for Affection and Approval

I see many people (both men and women) who complain that their Other is not sufficiently affectionate and doesn't voluntarily give them words of praise, encouragement, approval, and appreciation. "She never kisses me when I come home from work." "He never tells me he loves me." "She never notices when I mow the lawn but only carps when the grass gets higher than she likes." (I hope your alarm buttons are buzzing from these "nevers.") "He hasn't told me I look pretty for months and months." Possibly all these Others really are cold and critical people. However, the underlying dynamic in all the examples is that the complainers were looking to their Others to supply their needs for affection and had pinned their feelings of self-worth onto their Others' grudging approval or nonapproval of them. This is giving your power away. Each of us needs—by journaling, self-observation, and exercises—to learn to love and appreciate ourselves. The person who "needs love" is the least apt to get it. And the person who is constantly asking approval ("Did I do this right?" "Do you think my hair looks nice this way?" "Do you think my presentation is good enough?") is apt to weary even the most devoted Other, who may then allow her sadistic subpersonality to come out with a sarcastic or critical remark. So before you indict your Other for being critical and unloving, examine what you may be doing to set yourself up for this behavior.

If you haven't learned how to give yourself the love and appreciation you are seeking in your Other, here's an exercise for you:

Fairy Godmother Exercise

Sit comfortably.

Take a few Complete Breaths.

Pretend that you are being visited by your own fairy godmother. Notice what she looks like, what she is wearing, the expression on her face. (If she doesn't look at you lovingly, she's not your fairy godmother! Dismiss her and visualize a truly loving person.)

Now BE the fairy godmother.

Tell your godson or goddaughter how much you love them, what great people they are. Tell them all the things you admire about them.

Assure them of your continuing presence, love, and approval.

Moral Indignation

Moral indignation is an attitude that originates in a person's expectations of Others, plus the desire to control or dictate their behavior.

Henry came to see me, morally indignant because his sister-in-law, he had discovered, was cheating on his older brother. Henry had idealized this couple and their marriage and *expected* them to continue forever as a model for him of how a marriage could be.

I sometimes have moral indignation problems when I discover that someone that I have trusted has been lying to me. In addition to the *expectation* that I have been having that this person will tell the truth, there is a subpersonality problem.

It goes like this: I am a reasonably honest and reliable person. If I say I will do something, you can count on me to do it. I very seldom lie. These behaviors are by choice, since I feel better living this way, and I don't feel especially "virtuous." But there's a shadow side of me that would like to lie and cheat and break promises with the best of the scoundrels. When I don't acknowledge this shadow side, or Scoundrel subpersonality, I can become highly indignant when others lie, cheat, steal, and break promises. I believe the most rabid of the post-Watergate Nixon-haters were those people who were out of touch with their own Scoundrel subpersonalities. Which is not to say that Nixon's behavior is to be condoned, but that the moral indignation that some people displayed was excessive and not good for their own mental health.

When you associate with people whose value systems are very different from yours, you have a choice. You can be critical, judgmental, morally indignant, and possibly engage in stormy debates with them. Or you can pretend that you are a Visiting Field Anthropologist and without judgment observe the sayings and behaviour of this interesting culture which doesn't happen to be yours. Note what values the people hold and the benefits they seem to derive from their belief systems. This is a favorite technique which I had developed while visiting some racist friends-of-the-family. As a teenager, I had argued and raved and ranted in some misguided missionary attempt to change their belief system which, of course, didn't work. Now, as a Visiting Field Anthropologist, I can spend peaceful time with them, appreciate them as they are, and spare my adrenals and my blood pressure.

Unfinished Business with Another Other

Vera came to see me feeling very unhappy that she had sent her lover packing for what had seemed at the time an excellent reason: He wasn't giving her as much affection and attention as she had wanted. Once he was gone, however, she missed him and bitterly regretted her actions. After some work she realized that her situation with her lover felt like a painful echo of her childhood situation with her mother. She had wanted to reject her mother ("If you won't love me the way I want you to love me, get away, don't touch me!") and hadn't dared. In her need to finish an old, unfinished situation, she had picked on the wrong person at the wrong time.

It is a common occurrence that men and women who haven't finished with their former spouses and lovers will transfer these feelings to new situations and people. Helen expects her new husband to criticize her cooking and so makes counteroffensive remarks about her cooking that leave the poor man puzzled and cautious. Frank's first wife ran away with another man and under California community property law was awarded half of his business; so Frank assumes his second wife might wish to do the same and asks her to sign a premarital agreement that would leave her with not much more than the clothes on her back, should either of them decide to get a divorce. As a result, there is a lack of trust on both sides in this second marriage.

Saboteur and Victim Subpersonalities

Remember Olivia? Her Saboteur/Victim subpersonality was convinced that her husband would leave her after their second child was born and so she interpreted every action of her husband to fit her theory, as well as attempting to promote some script-fulfilling incidents.

Whenever you feel that your Other is treating you badly, do some self-observation to ascertain whether there is a part of you that is sabotaging situations (making it possible for him to do these dreadful things) or enjoying being a Victim. What part of you enjoys what is happening? What part of you stands to profit by the continuance of whatever it is you are complaining about with your Other?

The hard probability is that until you start being straight with yourself and become fairly skillful in the art of **self-observation**, you can pretty much expect to have some major difficulties in your relationships with other people. Is the answer then to go live in the desert and be a hermit until you reach the ideal state of mind? Heavens, no! Paradoxically, the fact is that one of the best laboratories for learning how to observe oneself and how to become straight and clear is in psychological relationship with others. We are all each others' teachers. The difficulties we have in relating with others furnish a mirror by which we may see ourselves more clearly. Only through relationship with others can we define our psychological boundaries. Those who do not take relationships seriously probably do not take themselves seriously, either. So now let's talk about some positive things we can do in relationships that we do take seriously.

Requests, Demands, and Contracts

Many people either don't know how or refuse to ask for the goodies they want from their Significant Others. A statement of the wish and a request are too simple and direct for them. So they may hint. A spouse may express a longing for a certain material item by leaving clipped advertisements or opened catalogs in strategic spots around the house. A child may pull her parent to the store window that holds the coveted object. Some people play guessing games: "You'll never guess what . . ." Some people hint by mirror behavior. In love-making, one partner may pet the other in the manner that he hopes his partner will then adopt.

Some people discover that they are afraid to ask for things they want for fear they will be refused, and then will feel either hurt or rejected. "If you really love me, you will not deny my simple request." This is not a "simple request," but emotional blackmail. "If she really loved me, she'd know how much it means to me to have her fix my breakfast and she'd want to get up and do it."

Some people feel angry at being denied. By some complicated emotional bookkeeping, they feel that the world *owes* them compliance with requests. "I ask for things so seldom, I feel that when I *do* ask for something, I ought to get it." This is neurotic arithmetic and just another form of emotional blackmail. When "ought" enters in, the request becomes a demand. More about this later.

Some people hesitate to ask for what they want for fear of exposing themselves, becoming vulnerable. In small degree this expresses a fear of losing face or of destroying one's image. The seemingly popular young woman might be unwilling to ask her friends for companionship on a weekend "date night" and thus betray her lack of a male companion. A man who wants people to believe that his life is going very well may hesitate to reveal any emotional distress to friends or colleagues or to ask for their support.

This fear of being vulnerable, when experienced to an extreme degree, betrays a basic mistrust of others; that if others know your deepest needs and strongest longing, this knowledge will somehow be used against you. In some rare situations, it might be. You remember the rabbit's request in the Uncle Remus stories: "Whatever you do, Br'er Fox, *please* don't throw me in the briar patch." And the rabbit's mistrust of the treacherous fox was confirmed when he was thrown into the briar patch and thus effected his escape. However, in nonhostile relationships, it's more effective to state exactly what you want instead of the opposite of what you want. The Br'er Rabbit Syndrome can be self-defeating. To state what you wish, what you would like to have, is one of the most honest communications one person can make to another.

Some people won't state what they want unless they are pretty certain their requests will be granted because they fear they will "lose face." They are the victims of some neurotic personal bookkeeping equation that says that if the "requests made" side of the ledger outbalances the "requests granted" side, they are somehow a less worthy person than before. For these people, it is very important to be powerful and to have their requests granted at a snap of their fingers, like some oriental potentate in his harem. The executive with these dynamics will arrange to have himself surrounded by "yes men." The housewife who brags to her women friends that "Martin gets me everything I ever ask for" probably doesn't risk asking him for anything she is not certain he is willing or eager to provide.

There are some requestees who will see a demand in any request, however genuinely made. These are people who are essentially ungiving people, for whom the request "Can you tell me what time it is?" becomes an outrageously intrusive demand. Their typical weapon in interpersonal relationships (at which they are usually quite unsuccessful) is to label the other person as "demanding," thus hoping to intimidate the Other about making any requests. An extreme example of this would be the person who presents himself as "unable to say no," and therefore his loving partner should spare him the painful necessity of either saying NO or (even worse) saying YES when he wants to say NO but "can't." If you, as the loving partner, fall for this trap, you will find yourself squeezed, unwilling to express yourself or your wants for fear of engaging your partner's "inability to say NO" (which, of course, is his unwillingness to take responsibility for where he is and what he wants). He has been practicing just another form of emotional blackmail on you.

In a healthy relationship between two people, each is free to ask for what he wants from the other, and the requestee is free to say *yes* or *no* to the request, according to *her* wants. And the relationship goes on whether the request is granted or not, with no hard feelings from the requestee that the request was made of her, and with no hard feelings from the requester, should his request meet with a *no*.

True asking is saying what you really want. NOT what somebody else wants you to ask for. NOT what you think you are entitled to. NOT what you think is an acceptable request.

There was some clear advice given on the action of asking and its rewards in the Sermon on the Mount:

> Ask and it shall be given you; seek, and ye shall find;
> knock, and it shall be opened unto you: For everyone
> that asketh, receiveth; and he that seeketh, findeth;
> and to him that knocketh, it shall be opened.

Jesus was talking, of course, about how to find the Kingdom of Heaven, and not how to get along with other people or how to gain material possessions. A misunderstanding of these lines may be part of the origin in our present culture for the neurotic notion that all requests will (or should) be granted. I'd like to rephrase these lines to make them applicable to more earthly requests:

> Ask, and you may very well receive. Knock, and
> sometimes the door will be opened for you. Certainly
> it's more likely to be opened if you knock than if
> you stand silently outside hoping that those within
> will ESP your presence and your desire.

When is a request not a request? When is a request a demand? A genuine request is a statement of where the requester is and what he would like from the other person, a statement made in such a way that he is asking for an equivalent feeling statement from the other. *The requestee is equally free to say yes or no.*

Let's run that one through again. A request is an honest statement of your position and what you would like, made in such a way that the other person is free to accept or refuse, since you are asking him to give a feeling statement of his position and what he would like.

A request is not a request but a demand if you let the other person know in any way (and tone of voice will do nicely)—

That you expect a certain answer.

That you are entitled to a certain answer.

That you will feel angryhurtrejectedabandoned if your request is not granted.

These are all manipulations, forms of emotional blackmail. "Honey, would you mind taking out the garbage? I've taken it out every day this week and it's *really* heavy." (*Translation:* Honey, you're unfeeling and unfair if you don't take out the garbage this time.)

"Mom, can I go to the campout? All the other kids are going." (*Translation:* If you don't give me permission, you're a mean mother and you'll make me look like an oddball.)

"Joan, could you pick up my cleaning, and stop by the grocery store for some eggs—we're all out—and hey! the postoffice couldn't deliver this package I've got a notice for. Would you mind, since you're going out anyway?" (*Translation:* I'm ignoring the fact that it's an extra hour's errands, and expect you'll do it "on the way" without complaint.)

Exercise on Requests and Demands

Sit down with your Significant Other or with a friend who is willing to role-play him for you.

First, ask for something you want in a demanding and manipulative way.

See how you feel making this demand.

Find out how the other feels.

Now *make a request* for what you want, by stating how you feel and asking and listening for how the Other feels.

How does it feel to make a request?

The foregoing may seem to imply that demands are bad. Not necessarily. Sneaky demands that masquerade as requests can be damaging to relationships. Straight, direct, legitimate demands are another matter.

If two people have a contractual arrangement whereby certain actions have been agreed upon in advance, it is quite legitimate to demand performance of those actions. That is, to ask for the specified part of the contract and expect to receive it. Our dollar bills used to say "Payable in silver *on demand* to the bearer." (They don't any more; the government changed its contract with us.) If a child has a weekly allowance, he may remind his parent that it's pay-up time and legitimately expect to be paid. Husbands and wives with sexually monogamous contracts demand and expect faithfulness from their spouses. If you come to see me for psychotherapy, I'll tell you my fees and expect to be paid.

We make contracts with one another whenever we come together for any length of time. The contracts can be explicit or implicit. Two people may explicitly contract to meet for lunch at the Golden Dawn at noon on Wednesday, October 3. One may understand the implicit contract to read that they are going "dutch"; the other may be intending to pick up the check for both.

An implicit contract that continues over a long period of time without discussion can acquire the substantial feeling of a written law. Perhaps on their first night in bed together, the woman takes the right side of the bed and the man the left. Twenty years later, if he ventures to get into bed on the right side, which is now HER side, she can feel all the outrage of violated territoriality. The examination of marital roles started by the women's liberation movement has caused us to examine many of the implicit contracts within marriage. Many wives are rebelling against the unspoken agreement made a decade or two ago that they are responsible for the purchase, preparation, and serving of the family food and are demanding some sharing of these tasks. Conversely, the husband, who for twelve years has been fulfilling his implicit contract to take out the garbage, may wish to have this contract changed. But if he just stops taking out the garbage, there may be some indignant words because his wife will probably feel that he "should" take out the garbage and that she has a right to demand fulfillment of the unspoken contract. It would be better to acknowledge that there *has* been an implicit contract and to request a renegotiation: "I'm tired of always being the one to take out the garbage, and I'd like you to do it half the time."

Before I got married (considerably before the beginning of Women's Lib), I did a minor self-torture trip about how we would handle our money. My parents had argued a lot about money and I didn't like the idea of having to ask anyone, even my dearly beloved husband-to-be, for money. (I hope you've noticed that this is another example of Unfinished Business from the Past.) I was too nonassertive in those days to bring up the topic for discussion. However, I could have foreseen the resolution by observing the behavior of my husband's family. For when he came home from work the first week, he handed me his paycheck just as his father had always given his to his wife.

And so, without any conversation on the subject, we established the implicit contract by which I handled the money, paid the bills, balanced the checkbook, and filled out the income tax returns.

Every marriage contract or living-together contract is unique. Couples continually create their own special rules for living together. The more explicit each partner is about his wants, and about his changing wants, the less friction there is apt to be in the relationship.

To help you identify the terms of your contract, or your rules for living together, let's do this exercise:

Ideal Future Contract Exercise

Imagine that Margaret Mead's suggestion of marriage as a renewable contract has been adopted. Your contract period is up, your old contract is finished, and you can now write a new contract.

What new conditions do you want written into this contract?

What old conditions do you want to keep?

Where do you want to live?

Who will be responsible for which household tasks? For the children? For pets?

How will you spend your money? Your leisure time? Your longer vacations?

Whose responsibility will it be to accept, reject, and extend invitations? (In other words, will one of you be the Czar in Charge of Social Life, or will this be a shared responsibility?)

Who will work outside the home . . . where . . . how many hours?

What about sex? (Frequency, variety, timing, on whose initiative, etc.)

What will you eat? When? Where?

When is bedtime? (And do you have to have synchronicity here?)

Be sure to specify pet peeves and idiosyncratic necessities; i.e., special pillow, fresh air in bedroom, no loud noise after 11 p.m., no smoking, or whatever.

And finally: Who carries out the garbage and how long do you want this new contract to run?

Here is an ice-breaker exercise for those couples who have difficulty in asking each other for the things each wants from the Other.

Satisfying Secret Needs

1. Each of you independently write a list of all the things that you would like to have done for you. Be sure to include all those items that you never dared to ask of anyone.

2. Share your lists orally and alternately, one person sharing one item, then the second person sharing one item, and so on.

3. When you have completed sharing your lists, each one of you say how he feels about the Other's list.

4. Set dates for two Needs-Satisfying evenings. Each evening, one person will be catered to by the Other, who will choose from the list those wishes he would enjoy gratifying. (The ones he doesn't want to do . . . or possibly can't do . . . he ignores without guilt.) On the second evening, the positions are reversed. This works much better when done on separate occasions. It's OK for the caterer to be creative and add some new items, but be sure you think your Other would enjoy them and that you're not just gratifying your own desires. It's best for the cateree to lie back, accept, and enjoy, without trying to reciprocate in any way.

Conflicting Requests

Aha! you say. Suppose Sue and I make our requests of each other and there's a conflict. I want to go to the movies tonight and she's had a hard day at the office and wants to stay home. What then? You can decide on a scale of one to ten how important it is for you to see that movie, on that night, and accompanied by Sue. Sue can ask herself the two magic questions and decide whether the movie invitation revives her energy level enough so that she wants to go. If she doesn't, you can postpone the movie, go alone, or go with someone else. Only by talking it out and being consciously aware of any demands, implicit contracts, or sneaky control trips can you come to a decision that will be pleasing to both of you. Is this a film that either of you feels is important for you to see together? Is it OK for you to go out in the evening without Sue? Do you always have to do everything together? (Dear God, let's hope you *don't* have one of those Siamese-twin type of relationships!) Do you "take turns" deciding how you will spend your time together? (If so, be sure that the end result is not that each of you is doing something she doesn't want to do 50 per cent of the time.) Beware of compromises that create situations pleasing to neither. Patty and Stewart could not agree on where to spend their summer vacation. She wanted to go to the midwest to visit her old home town and attend her high school reunion. He wanted to go to Hawaii and swim and snorkel. So they did neither, but went camping with mutual friends and both had a miserable, resentful time.

How do *you* resolve such conflicts with your Others?

Conflicts are inevitable in any close relationship. (Watch out for the child who is "never any trouble" to his parents, or for the marriage where the partners never disagree. There's probably an explosion in the making.) *How* those conflicts get resolved is probably the critical factor in determining whether or not the relationship will be a mutually satisfying, deep, and truly intimate one.

Communication Games

If you and a Significant Other (which could be a spouse, lover, child, parent, sibling, even a boss) are having problems, failing to communicate, finding it difficult to talk to one another, or feeling uncomfortably distant from each other, it makes sense to call in a third party to help you to talk and to hear one another. This could be a psychotherapist, a marriage counselor, a family therapist, or even an objective friend.

You could also agree together to play one or more of the following structured communication games. In all of these games, you are to sit facing one another and look each other in the eyes. Another rule is to listen carefully when the other person is speaking and not interrupt him. If you have a tape recorder, it might be useful to tape the sessions so that you can play them back afterwards together.

1. The "I Want" Game: Each of you takes turns saying a sentence to the Other that starts with "I want." Each listens to the Other's "I want" and then states her own "I want." Don't get derailed by discussions, arguments, or justifications about any of the wants. Just make a fairly rapid alternate sharing of each of your wants. These can range from goods and services that you want from the Other ("I want you to take out the garbage every night," "I want a new pair of jeans," etc.) to goals you want for yourself ("I want to finish my degree," "I want to live in Arizona when I retire," "I want to get an 'A' in French this term." "I want to sell our big house and move to a small apartment.") Hearing another's want may remind you of your opposite want!

In an atmosphere of unimpeded and uncensored disclosure you will discover new things you never suspected about your Significant Other. When he says, "I don't want to invite the Robbins to our next party," she may forget the rules to exclaim: "Neither do I! I thought we always invited them because *you* wanted them!"

This is a game for two or more players. If the whole family plays, it's important to follow the rule of everyone speaking in turn until all the wants are stated. If your want involves someone who is present, state it directly to that person: "Henry, I want you to remember to sign out where you are going on the message board," rather than "I want everyone to sign out on the message board," (when Henry is the only person who consistently forgets to do so). When the game is finished, feel free to discuss your feelings about any of the Others' wants.

2. The "I Resent" Game: Again, each of you takes turns saying to the Other sentences that start with "I resent." The Other will listen to his partner without interruption and then state his own "I resent." These resentments can be resentments against the Other or outside resentments. (Or you might want to make the rule that only resentments against the Other will qualify.) For this exercise I would set the timer for five minutes and then discuss what you are feeling.

If this game is played with all the family, it's important not to make one person into a scapegoat. It's hard to make a specific rule here; just be sensitive. If the last two resentments have been directed toward Ed and your turn is next, even if you have a great smoldering "I resent" for Ed, it would be more useful for you to select another family member so Ed would not feel ganged up on. Whenever the whole family picks on one person as causing "the problem in the family," it's probably time for family therapy and some objective sorting out of what is happening, with a competent psychotherapist.

Regardless of the number of players, the "I resent" game should definitely be counterbalanced with the next game.

3. The "I Appreciate" Game: Start your sentences with "I appreciate" and tell your Other (alternately) what you appreciate about her and also what you appreciate about your life in general. If you are playing this game with the whole family, you might focus on one person at a time with all family members contributing at least one appreciation.

These are the three most important games. Some others are:
        4. "I feel you don't understand . . ."
        5. "I get angry with you when . . ."
        6. "I feel happy with you when . . ."
        7. "I want you to know . . ."

Increasing Your Intuitive Knowledge of Your Other

Relationships seem to flow most smoothly when people have a strong intuitive knowledge of each other. The father on an impulse buys his son a model airplane, which was something the boy had just started wanting. The wife produces a misplaced object just as her husband starts looking for it. These kinds of knowledge of the Other cannot be consciously learned; it seems to be the work of the right side of the brain, which perceives things in wholes and symbols and not in the logical, cause-and-effect manner of the left side. The following exercise, however, may generate some symbols that can promote two people's intuitive understanding of each other.

Intuition Exercise

Sit facing each other.

Take turns each revealing to the Other some things you believe he does not know about you (between five and ten rounds).

Now close your eyes. Let symbols emerge for you about your Other, specifically:

        a. What color?
        b. What flower?
        c. What animal?
        d. What tool?
        e. What sound?
        f. What architectural form?
        g. What mythological person
           or object?

You do not have to explain, justify, or defend your choices, even to yourself. Just let them emerge. Write them down.

Now open your eyes. Share your lists with each other. Share your feelings. For instance, if your partner, who is pretty unknowledgeable about tools, sees you as an electric drill, and this is your very favorite tool, tell her so. And indulge in a paean of praise for the versatility, durability, agility, and velocity of the electric drill so that she can know more about the symbol that she chose, as well as understand some of the attributes that you value.

Love

> Love is not what you think.
> —Jessamyn West

Unfortunately, most people that I see are not asking how to learn to love but are asking how to get Others to love them. And, readers, I have no magic answers for the second request. I don't know of any mechanical or material ways to cause someone to love you. And if you believe you have found some, beware. The result is probably not real love but a transitory possessive attachment to your physical beauty, or your attentiveness, or your cooking, or your sexiness, or your gifts, or your wit. And you will find that you are not truly loved the minute you do not fulfill his demands or her expectations.

Love is the flower of freedom. If you try to capture it and hold it, it will surely die as any flower that is cut and put into a vase or any butterfly that is captured and pinned to a board.

Love that is pursued will not be caught.

Love blooms only when no demands are made.

Love vanishes when comparisons are made.

Love cannot be held or guarded like money you deposit in your bank account, in anticipation of a future withdrawal.

No insurance company will write you a policy on the continuance of love.

Joel Kramer writes that love "comes only when there is an innocence that puts away all hopes and expectations, all flatteries and insults, all memories. It comes only when there is a stillness so that I may see you."

Pause here and observe your reactions to what I've written so far about love.

It would be more useful for people to ask how to learn to love. This is more teachable; also, it is more rewarding to love than to be loved, although this is very difficult for some people to comprehend. Being loved by someone whom you do not love can be a heavy burden.

The way to learn to love is to start observing yourself as you are in your relationship with your Other. Do you accept him as he is, or are you busy designing how he should change? Do you expect her to do certain things for you, to love you in return, perhaps? Do you fear that future time when your relationship with him will end? Do you make demands on your Other? Notice how all these attitudes and actions obstruct the birth of love.

There's no point in making New Year's resolutions not to demand or not to fear. A resolution not to demand is creating a new demand. Your decision not to fear could be motivated by fear of never finding love. Rather, watch what it is you are doing in relationship, watch the effects of what you do, and make your minute-by-minute choices very consciously.

Notice whether you are totally relating with your Other *now*. Or are you comparing the current flow with past times in your relationship? Or anticipating future events with your Other? Love does not come until you abandon yourself into the present, forsaking all preoccupations with past and future. It comes without warning or heraldry; all of a sudden, you are in the middle of it. And if you stop to say, "Hey, this is great, I want to hang onto this!", it will have already gone away.

Jealousy

If your Other is jealous of you, that should be your clearest proof that you are not loved. (This is the reverse of the thinking that prevailed in my high school set, but then we were a rather immature lot.) Glenn said, and believed, that he loved Sheila very much, so much that he couldn't stand the thought of her being with another man. Sheila constantly assured him that she loved only him and never even thought of other men, much less spent time with any of them. Glenn's jealousy finally got so great that he started driving her to and from work to minimize the possibility of contact with other men. Next, he worried about what might be happening during those hours at work, so he questioned her at length every evening about any conversations with male coworkers that day. Glenn was too out of touch with his real feelings to know that his possessiveness (not love!) of Sheila stemmed from feelings of great insecurity which he was unwilling to admit. Additionally, there was a part of him that wanted to have a freer marriage and to have conversations and relationships with other women. This subpersonality was so completely disowned by Glenn that he projected it onto Sheila, accusing her of all the desires that were really his.

Since jealous people are typically so unaware of what they are doing and what they are truly feeling, they are most in need of working with a therapist who will help them become aware of those denied areas and their projections onto others.

Exercise on Jealousy

Find a place where you can be alone and a time when you will feel unhurried.

Sit comfortably.

Take several Complete Breaths.

Review your marriage or current love relationship or a relationship that has ended. List for yourself all the occasions on which you felt jealous when you thought that—
    he was interested in someone else
    she found someone else more attractive/sexy/intelli-
       gent/fun/compassionate than you
    he was getting more attention than you
    she was having an affair with someone else
    he was giving more credence to his family's—friends'
      —colleagues'—opinions than he was to yours.
(Have you noticed that these all involve Comparison Trips?)

Now take each incident singly and deliberately try it on for size. See if *you* were interested in someone else; see if you knew someone who was more attractive, sexy, etc., than your Other. Did you want to have the kind of fun you fantasized he was having?

Now examine the ways in which you scared or prohibited yourself from doing or getting what you wanted.

Most jealousy is a paranoid projection, an attribution to the Other of behavior or feelings that are really your own but that you are afraid to claim because of moral scruples or fear of failure or other reasons. This is an example of the shadow side of the personality. If you are having jealous feelings toward any of your friends, this is a particularly good time to keep track of your dreams and to write in your journal.

Sex, Sex, Sex

Stop right now, and notice your reaction to this subchapter heading. Is this an area of particular interest for you? In fact, have you skipped other sections in favor of reading this one? Would you say that sex is a problem for you? Is sex a joyful pastime?

Ideally, sexuality is a very natural, inevitable, and flowing part of the union between people who are involved in an intimate love relationship. However, this natural flow has been crippled in the West, first by the repressive mores of Judeo-Christian religion and Victorian society and, more recently, by the sexual revolution itself. The contemporary focus on sexuality as an end in itself has caused many of us to lose sight of the needs of the total person.

Our language reflects our changed attitudes. Many people don't talk about "making love" any more. Instead, they "have sex." This signals the danger, this simple change from a verb to a noun. It's no longer a process, a doing, a happening, but an acquisition, an accomplishment. We now have sex, just as we have a Volvo, or a Pentax, or a new stereo. And the nouns are modified by adjectives. We don't just have sex, but we have "good" sex and we have "bad" sex. And we make comparisons: "Sex with Jim is better than sex with Bob."

When you make sex into an object, then your partner becomes an object, too: "Susie is one of the best lays I've ever had." This is the kind of derogatory talk that women have historically objected to, and rightfully so. But in recent years, women themselves have adopted this same locker-room attitude that used to be more characteristic of men, as one of the less desirable gifts from the women's liberation movement. Women now feel free to get together and gossip about men: who has the best staying power, who delights in foreplay and, alas! who's frequently impotent. Perhaps the greatest misuse of sexuality is this encouragement to view each other as objects and not as an I and a Thou.

Making sexuality an end in itself, and therefore something to be pursued brings us to this paradox: Sex delight is like happiness; it does not come when pursued. The way to have the Big Orgasm is NOT to plan for it, wait for it, expect it, and watch to see if it's going to happen now . . . or five minutes from now.

Back in the days when I was smoking marijuana, I frequently had an experience that caused me some concern about myself until I understood what was happening. My lover and I would make love and I would experience this cataclysmic event that I would afterwards realize must be an orgasm. However, it felt like such a totally new, original, unique experience that I would immediately feel that I must be some sort of phony or fraud to think that I had ever experienced orgasm before, much less attempted to instruct others how to achieve one, and especially if I accepted their payment for this instruction! I felt as humbled as I felt fake and defrocked. After this same experience, with its aftermath of wondering and self-recrimination had happened a few times, I caught on to what was really happening. When you are totally in the present, when you *totally* give yourself to making love, then there are no previous orgasmic experiences available for comparison, and each orgasm is truly a first orgasm, a new experience.

The Fallacy of Having Rules for Sex

In the first phase of the sexual revolution (the 1920's, 30's and 40's), the sex manuals suggested two rules in order to have "good" sex: the simultaneous orgasm and the transfer from clitoral orgasm to "vaginal orgasm." Both were a lot of hogwash.

Some best-selling sexpert of the 30's proclaimed that the ultimate ecstasy was supposedly achieved when the man and the woman had their orgasms simultaneously, so the couple should always try to pace themselves to reach this goal. The faster partner should slow down, and the slower partner should speed up. God knows how many couples devalued perfectly fine lovemaking experiences because they hadn't satisfied this criterion for ultimate ecstasy.

As for the kind of orgasm required, women were taught to feel immature, somehow inferior, and definitely not feminine if they had only clitoral orgasms. They had to make the magic transfer to a "vaginal orgasm" to become real women. So strong was this genital mystique that few women (none in my circle in the 50s) had the courage to say, "The emperor is naked, he's not wearing any clothes. I don't have vaginal orgasms and I wonder whether you do, either." We can be grateful that Masters and Johnson have liberated us from that myth.

Having a goal . . . any goal . . . is going to put people in their heads, make a task out of sex, and deprive them of the pleasure for which they were ostensibly searching. That's the paradox.

Bhagwan Shree Rajneesh writes,

> The more modern man feels incapable of going deep in sex, the more he thinks about it. It becomes a vicious circle. The more he thinks about it, the more it becomes cerebral. Then even sex becomes futile . . . a repetitive thing—boring.

There was an interesting study done in the early sixties by John Cuber and Peggy Harroff. They interviewed a large number of successful Americans—prominent businessmen, government leaders, professionals, artists—and found that for the majority of their subjects, sex was "almost nonexistent, something to be stifled." Sex was primarily seen as tension release, something to be "performed"—a "necessary nuisance"—with as little "fanfare" as possible. A quote from one subject: "Like any other body function, it needs attention from time to time."

Stop now and notice what you are feeling. Is sex ever just a tension release for you? A necessary nuisance?

Or is it something you enjoy or think you would enjoy but believe you don't do very well?

The Disastrous Pursuit of the Great O

One of the things accomplished by the sexual revolution is that we're now free to talk about sex, discuss sex, compare sex. So there's a spate of books about how to do it and—unfortunately—how to do it better. While there is useful information in a few of them, the overriding message in most of them is, "Look at all the great times these sensuous people are having!

Are you having such good times?" And then they specify an orgasm every time you make love, or the woman having *x* number of orgasms, or the man's staying power being a range of *x* to *y* minutes, etc. If you don't measure up to these standards, you should try this and this technique, and then you'll have good times like the people described in the books. The end result is that the reader feels inferior; and in his next sexual encounter he spends most of his time in his head trying to remember the technique, rather than putting his awareness into his groin where the action is.

I wish one writer in particular had taken a general semantics course before he wrote a sex manual, because his favorite words are "every," "never," and "always." "Every woman does have . . ." According to him and all too many other sexperts, *every* woman should have an orgasm. It's not only her inalienable right (and I'm not quarreling with this first part), but it's also her duty during the orgasm to make her man feel manly by squealing with pleasure. So we see many a woman who used to enjoy the sexual union with her partner now feeling either cheated or inferior, and she starts in pursuit of what I call the Great O. Then, provided she doesn't get too hung up in the pursuit, she learns to have an orgasm (maybe through therapy, maybe by masturbating with a vibrator, maybe by *Kegeling**, maybe by her partner's learning better how to stimulate her, maybe by learning to flow into it). Further, she may set for herself the standard of an orgasm every time, or worse, "I have to have my orgasm with intercourse. Finger-fucking and cunnilingus don't count." Is sex a sport, a ball-game, that we must have such rules?

The next thing that may happen is that she hears Amelia in her women's group describe these great multiple orgasms that she has. Or she may read Mary Jane Sherfey, who says that women are potentially insatiable and can have six or more

---

* After Arnold Kegel, M.D., who developed exercises for strengthening the pubo-coccygeal (PC) muscle for women with urinary incontinence. Since this muscle also contracts during orgasm, Kegel's patients developed some interesting fringe benefits as they learned to know and control their PC muscle. The basis exercise: Contract the muscle for three seconds (imagine you are stopping the flow of urine), then relax it for another three, and so on for ten times. You can practice your *Kegeling* anywhere undetected, and it's great fun in dull staff meetings.

orgasms with intravaginal coition or up to fifty or more orgasms in an hour's time with clitoral-area stimulation. Those are big numbers! If she continues this game, she may start devaluing the single satisfactory orgasm she has been having, in pursuit of more—more! And her man may be the sort of person who encourages her and gets some kind of a kick out of playing the numbers game with her.

I once had a lover who counted, and when I found out that he was counting, I felt intruded upon as if by a Peeping Tom. I would have preferred that he stay with his own pleasure, rather than trying to calibrate mine.

Stop again and take stock. Does any of the above apply to you? I've been describing one of the most common subversions of the normal sexual flow—viewing sex as performance. When sex is used as a means to any other ends, you can expect that it will be less joyful, less fulfilling than when it happens as a natural organismic process. Let's talk about some common misuses of natural sex.

Sex as Performance

This is a very large category. It includes the woman who has to have bigger and better and more numerous orgasms, and the man who has to prove how great he is by "giving" them to her. Or the woman who fancies herself an accomplished lover the equal of a trained courtesan. In Gael Greene's *Blue Skies, No Candy*, the heroine fantasizes that she receives an Oscar for her superior blow jobs. Enough said! Each of us is responsible for our own orgasms. You're in charge here, too.

Sex as an Antidote for Loneliness

Sex can be used as a tradeoff by people who don't really want to make love but are terrified of being alone, as this excerpt from Dory Previn's "the lady with the braid" portrays:

> would you care to stay till sunrise
> it's completely your decision
> it's just that going home is such a ride . . .
> going home is such a low and lonely ride
> would you hang your denim jacket
> near the poster by picasso

do you sleep on the left side or the right?
would you mind if I leave on the light . . .?
shall I make you in the morning
a cup of homemade coffee?
I will sweeten it with honey and with cream
when you sleep
do you have dreams?
you can read the early paper
and I can watch you while you shave . . .
would you care to stay till sunrise
it's completely your decision
it's just the night cuts through me
like a knife
would you care to stay awhile
and save my life . . .?

Sex because You Want to Start a Relationship with Someone

This is more typically a woman's trip, but not exclusively so
by any means. Kathy, for instance, is a single woman in her
early 30s, lonely, feeling incomplete and unworthy and quite
desperate to "have a relationship" with a man. She has a behavior that she repeats over and over. When she feels particularly lonely, she goes to one of the many singles bars in the city,
meets a young man, and either takes him to her apartment or
goes to his. Before she knows very much about him, much less
how she feels about him in the deepest places of her being, she
is in bed with him and having sex. Not making love. Having
sex. The next day she feels confused and a little icky about the
whole episode. She waits for the phone to ring. If he calls, she
feels better and somehow vindicated. Perhaps this will develop
into a relationship after all. If he doesn't call, her basic feelings
of self-unworth magnify. She may make mistakes at the office
and feel incapable of working on some new project that she was
supposed to develop. She may pick a fight with her mother on
the long-distance phone. In an attempt to cure her bad feelings
about herself, she goes back to the Lonely Hearts pub another
night and picks up another young man. And so on. The only
real cure is when she learns to become aware of her feelings,
to listen to what her body and her thoughts and her feelings are
telling her, and then to say NO to men on those occasions when

it's just not right for her to be sexually intimate. There are no moral rules here, only **self-observation** and the knowledge of her own deepest nature.

Sex as Duty

This may have been the most prevalent misuse of the sexual act. The myth used to be that women didn't enjoy sex but engaged in it because it was their marital duty. I love the story of the Victorian bride whose mother tells her on her wedding night that she must submit to her husband, it is her duty; and advises her to lie back quietly, shut her eyes, and think of England!

How about you? Are there times when you "have sex" not because you want to, but because you think it is your duty? With the sexual revolution and the women's liberation movement, most Americans . . . men and women . . . should be able to answer "no" to this one.

A variation is *Prescription Sex.* For example, Myrna and Dick make love infrequently. Dick goes to his doctor because of prostatitis and the doctor tells him he needs to have more frequent intercourse or he's going to have a real medical problem with his prostate . . . So Dick goes home and hands the prescription to Myrna.

Sex for Security's Sake

Joe will often respond to Jane's advances when he's tired and would really rather go to sleep because he is afraid she will leave him if he doesn't keep her sexually satisfied. Susannah often initiates sex when her man is about to go off on a trip because she wants him to remember how sexy she is so he won't stray into other pastures while he's gone. The extreme version of Security Sex is the woman who would really prefer never to have sex with her husband but enjoys the standard of living he gives her and would hate to have to go to work.

This is similar to out-and-out *Mercenary Sex,* which is given to someone—either a man or a woman—in direct exchange for money, gifts, food, a part in a film, a promotion, and so on.

Social-Climbing Sex is a subtle version of Mercenary Sex. This involves bedding down with someone of a higher social class than you, so you can meet groovier people and go to parties where the Beautiful People go. In *Trophy Sex* you select your bed partners for their name-dropping currency.

Sex as Reassurance

This is a very large category. The classic example is the aging man who gets reassured about his youth and virility when he gets it on with a woman young enough to be his daughter. But women, too, have Reassurance Sex. Marcia, phobic about turning forty, beds down every willing and attractive man who crosses her path to reassure herself that she's still young enough to be desirable.

Sex as a Cure for Nostalgia

Pat knew he was not in love with Grace any more, and he did not want to revive the relationship. But he kept remembering their good times in bed and thought that perhaps if he slept with her again he could finally get her out of his thoughts . . . A related sex-for-other-ends is *Sex to Satisfy Your Curiosity* (more euphemistically known as Discovery Sex). You're curious to know what a certain person is like, you're intrigued, you're fascinated. And there's no better place to find out who another person is than in bed, right?

I hope you've been considering your own sexual behavior as you've been reading this past section. Let's do an exercise to make your observations specific:

Recapitulation of Your Sexual History

Think back over your past sexual involvements. Which ones evolved into sexual intimacy in the natural flow of events?

Which ones were undertaken by you for other ends?

Which were most satisfying? (Observe in this memory recall; don't judge.)

Examine your current sexual involvement. Do you make love? Or have sex?

Are you aware of any other ends—Reassurance, Duty, Security, Antidote for Loneliness, and so on?

Do you make love to make love or to pursue the Great O?

The really important point here is to learn to observe yourself, to include your sex life in your Evening Review in order to learn what you really want for yourself and have that emerge.

The Power of Unconditional Love

As part of the art of self-observation you will learn to notice when you are making judgments about others. You might first notice a thought ("How stupid of him to have said that.") or a feeling ("I hate her when she gives that silly laugh"), and then further self-observe, "I'm making a judgment." If the answer to your second magic question is, "I don't want to judge, I want to accept him the way he is," then you are well on the road to learning how to love unconditionally. This is the kind of love that the major world religions talk about; I'm discussing it now not to preach but to acquaint you with a powerful tool for freeing yourself from the most important unpleasant emotions.

In unconditional love you permit yourself to love the essence, or Self, of each Other unconditionally—that is, with total acceptance and no judgments. This does not mean that you approve of all his actions and behaviors, but you do accept *him*. The old Quaker maxim, "Condemn the action but never the actor," is a useful motto to help discriminate the difference. This means that you may hate the way your mother raised you (and resolve to raise your children differently) and still love your mother. Sometimes you need to put yourself into your mother's moccasins to learn to understand how she could have treated you the way she did. Most important, you need to forgive her for those actions.

Forgiveness is not an admission that she was right in what she did, but it is a statement that you understand the frailty of the person who injured you. And to perceive that you could have (and possibly have) been capable of the same actions. Forgiveness implies an acceptance of the imperfection of human behavior and an acknowledgment of this for you, your mother, and anyone else whom you feel has injured you or done you an injustice. To forgive a person, you remove the conditions you have placed upon her which prevent you from loving her unconditionally:

Exercise on Unconditional Love

Sit comfortably.

Take a few Complete Breaths.

Picture one by one the important people you have known throughout your life—parents, siblings, teachers, friends, lovers, spouse, children, etc.

Say to each person: "I love you unconditionally. I accept you just the way you are." Be aware of how you feel as you say this.

When you find a person for whom you cannot say this with complete honesty, notice the conditions you have put on that person. "You should have been kinder to me," "You shouldn't have criticized me," and so on.

Now put yourself in the other person's place. See if you can understand why he was not very kind or why she criticized. What was going on in that person's life at that time?

Now return to yourself and see if you can say honestly, "I forgive you for _____ and I remove this as a condition for not loving you unconditionally. I now love you unconditionally and accept you just the way you are."

What is your reaction to this exercise?

Did you discover many people whose essence you do not love unconditionally?

Did you identify the conditions you had placed on them?

If there are conditions which you refuse to remove, what are they and how do you feel about them?

Most important, are there conditions you put onto your own love for yourself?

When I first did this exercise, I was surprised to find a person in my far-distant past against whom I had an unsuspectedly deep grudge. I wrestled and wrestled with trying to forgive her and kept colliding with my demand: "Because you were a minister's wife, you should have had more Christian charity and not have done such and such."* However, when I put myself in her place and imagined her upbringing and her life and her values, I came to a clear understanding of how she could have behaved as she did. And since then, I can honestly say that I love the memory of her unconditionally and feel much lighter with the loss of that bitter grudge I had been carrying.

"Trying" to forgive someone or criticizing yourself for being judgmental can hinder your development of the ability to love unconditionally. Again you need to self-observe. If your last self-observation was "Damn it, Mary, there you go again judging John. That's not unconditional love," your next observation might be: "Mary, now you're judging yourself and getting on your case about not being perfect. Yes, you were making a judgment about John. Good that you noticed. And what do you want to do *now*?"

The world religions teach that we need to love *all* our neighbors unconditionally in order to have good emotional and mental health. Neighbor, according to its Aramaic translation, means anyone of whom you are mentally aware. This would include everyone you see on the TV news or read about in your daily newspaper. What is your reaction to this definition of "neighbor" and to this scope for unconditional love?

Love, according to Erich Fromm, is not primarily a relationship to a certain Other or Others, but an attitude, an orientation that characterizes one's relatedness to the world as a whole. "If I truly love one person, I love all persons, I love the world, I love life." And conversely, love of one's family with no feeling for the stranger is a sign of a basic inability to love.

Stop now and assess how you are feeling about Fromm's statement and what you are thinking about this section on unconditional love.

---

* Since I have now truly forgiven her, I'm not going to label her behavior for you. Remembering those long bygone incidents and recounting them for you would be evidence that I had *not* forgiven her.

CHAPTER 4

ON KEEPING A JOURNAL

During my first hour with a new person I frequently will ask this seemingly nonapropos question: "Which color do you prefer, red, blue, or black?" And then I'll hand the startled person a book of blank pages bound in the color of his choice. First of all, it's fun to give a present to someone who's possibly sitting there worrying about fees. Secondly, it's thoroughly anti-psycho-analytic (giving a patient a gift? Come on!) Most important, it is a concrete demonstration to the person of the value that I place on keeping a journal.

I see the journal as one "place" that I (or anyone else) can always go to work out a current problem, to wrestle into articulate awareness a current feeling or mood, to record the *meaning* of a recent experience, to come to a decision.

In order for a journal to be maximally useful, it should be a place where you—the recorder—can be completely honest. And for that reason I would suggest that you write just for yourself, and never with the thought of showing it to your spouse, therapist, or anyone else. Whenever you write with the idea that another will someday read it, then you will start subtly slanting or selecting the material—to make you look good or to make him look bad or to let her know how much you suffer, etc. However, if, *after* you have written an entry, you find that you would like to show (or better, *read*) that entry to a particular person because it crystallizes your feelings so well, then do it. It's the writing-for-the-purpose-of-having-someone-read-your entries that I would like to caution you against. And don't leave your journal lying around in plain sight if you live with someone who is curious about or feels threatened by whatever is going on in your life. That's an invitation to snoop and also an incitement to you to do a sly disclosure via your written pages.

The word "journal" implies daily, but I would hate to see you make journal-writing into another "should." Rather, I'd prefer that you perceive the journal as a constantly available resource in which you can write as needed and wanted . . . which sometimes will be daily, sometimes weekly, and when under duress, even hourly!

Do date your entries—day, month, time of day, year. Even note the place. This will help you to recall more completely where you were when you made a particular entry. Rereading your journal can be of almost as much value as the initial writing of it. Without a written record, the memory plays tricks. This is one way to keep your record straight. It's amazing, when you reread large portions of your journal, how many themes will pop up that you never noticed while you were living that section of your life . . . always get a headache at staff meeting . . . recurrent fatigue . . . pleasure of being with Jim, etc. Perhaps you will notice recurrent patterns in your relationship with the opposite sex. Perhaps you will stumble onto a persistent impasse in your interactions with parents or children . . . and an obvious solution.

Most importantly, the journal can give you signposts on the path of your continuing growth. You may shudder as you read how badly you handled a certain situation or were torn apart by another experience, and yet it's very heartening to realize how much you have changed since those entries . . . how much better equipped you are to handle similar situations now.

Erica Jong's heroine, Isadora Wing, is a journal-keeper, and near the dénouement of *Fear of Flying* rereads her entries:

> As I read the notebook, I began to be drawn into it as into a novel. I almost began to forget that I had written it. And then a curious revelation started to dawn. I stopped blaming myself; it was that simple . . . It was . . . heartening to see how much I had changed in the past four years.

There's no right or wrong about what should go into your journal. Whatever you feel strongly about is a good guide. I frequently write about out-of-town workshops, particularly the ones where I feel quite high and have done some work that I think was innovative and don't want to forget. I worry that my memory is not as good as it "should" be (another kind of self-torture trip), so I'll frequently include names connected with high experiences that I want to remember: paintings, people, music, places.

I also . . . *still* . . . have trouble making decisions. Once I got sick on the eve of a trip to give two scheduled workshops. I didn't want to cancel, and went back and forth in my decision-making process until I got out my old faithful journal and listed the pros and cons in two different columns. Then I read these over and the fairly obvious choice emerged.

My first experience with this method was when I was thirteen and had to choose which parent I would live with. I can remember agonizing over the decision, then making two columns labeled "Living with Daddy" and "Living with Mother" on a sheet of paper and putting pluses or minuses after each item. Of course, I remember that it was Mother who won, but I've forgotten all the reasons and their weightings. It would be interesting to be able to reread that piece of paper now.

What to write about? Any experience that is heavily charged with feeling probably warrants inclusion. Falling in love. Being "hurt" by someone. (This is a particularly good one to do in detail. You may learn what *you* contributed to the situation.) Being angry. Feeling sad.

One of the ways I torture myself is to become upset that I might not be able to accomplish everything I feel I need to do by a certain deadline—a departure, say. So if you were to read my journal, you would find periodically a list of "Things to Do" —written to stop myself from fretting. And I can notice in rereading old journals that this need to make lists has abated only slightly.

Some items that bear investigation in the journal are your initial impressions of new people, places, jobs, etc. They, too, can be most instructive to reread at a later date. Are your first impressions valid? Then you can rely more on your intuitive first look. Or are these first impressions based on prejudices and stereotypes that dissipate as you know the person better? If so, perhaps your journal will teach you that you need to keep an open mind about new people and experiences, and collect more data before making assessments.

You might use your journal as a place to examine your relationship with someone whom you dislike. Write out a fancied dialogue between the two of you. You may discover that she is like one of your negative subpersonalities, a portion of yourself that you dislike.

If someone has disappointed or hurt you, write a position statement to him and address him by name. This will probably be one of those letters-that-never-get-mailed, but it will help you articulate how you feel, where you felt the other person was "wrong," and what you contributed to the situation. What expectations were you having of him, for example? You probably will emerge from your journal writing with a much clearer sense of what your values are and what's important for you.

If you're reading a book that seems particularly meaningful, you may want to transcribe those passages that are quoteworthy. This may sound laborious, yet the actual copying of material forces you to take a more in-depth look at the impressive passages. These quotes, embedded in the developing fabric of your life, will help to illuminate a particular period at a later rereading of your journal. I can now recapture my emotional experiences of the events of the teachers' strike at San Francisco State College in 1968–1969 far more accurately because of the inclusion of parallel feelings from Anaïs Nin about the Spanish Civil War thirty years earlier.

You can use your journal as a place where you can work to develop your awareness in many specific categories. For instance, eating. Perhaps you want to lose weight. Then record *everything* that goes into your mouth: how much, when, what you were feeling just before you decided to eat, how much you enjoyed the food, and how you felt afterwards. (For this you might want to have a small subjournal, small enough to carry with you everywhere. You can transcribe it into the main journal later.) You might want to weigh yourself each day, at the same time of day, and record that in your journal, too. Before too much time elapses you will be able to discover which foods and which amounts of food are advisable for losing, maintaining, or gaining weight. You will also notice what situations or fantasies trigger the desire to gorge. One of my people discovered that she went to the refrigerator every time she started thinking about all the great things she could have done with her life and hadn't. As a result of this realization, she painted a sign and hung it on the refrigerator: "This is the door to your refrigerator, not the door to success." The second time she caught herself about to quiet her frustrations with food, she slammed the refrigerator door shut, got in her car, drove to the local college and enrolled for the next quarter. Whatever you decide to do as a result of your new awareness of what/when/how you eat is up to you. YOU'RE IN CHARGE!

You can use record-keeping to increase your awareness of other forms of nourishment that you are taking in (or not taking in).

Frequently my group and I will observe that a particular member doesn't notice or "take in" compliments given to him by the others. Interestingly, these typically are the people who believe that others don't like them, don't respect them. I have suggested to them that they carry a small notebook with them and conscientiously record every compliment (both overt and implicit) given to them during the week. Their reports the next week usually reflect amazed pleasure at how well regarded they are by their associates and how frequently they are praised and appreciated.

If you think you smoke too much, and you think you want to stop, you can record your way to awareness and a responsible decision. Attach a small notebook or piece of paper to your pack of cigarettes. In the beginning don't cut back on your smoking, just honestly record how you *do* smoke. Note the time and the setting for every cigarette. What were you feeling and doing and thinking at the moment that you felt the urge for a cigarette? How satisfying was this particular cigarette on a scale of one to five? How much of it did you actually smoke? When you have established your baseline of awareness you may realize that certain cigarettes in the day are not all that enjoyable or that cigarettes smoked in certain surroundings are not that pleasurable (where you have to suffer the wrath of the nonsmokers, perhaps!) and so decide to eliminate these occasions.

You first need to determine what the goodies are that you get from smoking and find some other source for this nourishment before you can easily stop smoking altogether. Who is the subpersonality that needs to have you smoke? Dorothy discovered that she really wanted something to hold in her fingers and readily found some non-cancer-causing substitutes. Patricia realized that smoking made her feel grownup and attractive to men . . . and she still smokes in those male-female tension-laden circumstances. Ted became aware that he needs to inhale deeply and feel the smoke circulating throughout his lungs in order to feel alive and real; he hasn't found another way of feeling as real and still smokes several packs a day. These last two examples may not sound like success stories to you. If so, it's because you are carrying the judgment that these people *should* stop smoking. I believe you've missed the point. Patricia and Ted did their homework. They became aware of the meaning of their smoking for them and they made deliberate decisions based on that awareness. You may not approve of their decisions, but that's not the point. THEY'RE IN CHARGE!

You can use your journal in a similar way to play detective about your health. If you get headaches, what foods are they associated with? What feeling states precede the onset of a headache? You can observe in retrospect the events and feelings preceding catching a cold. Or getting tired.

Novelist Violet Weingarten kept a "journal about living with chemotherapy," in which she recorded the hopes and fears of the last two years of her life in which she "had (has) cancer." I infer from reading her journal that it was a helpful resource for her in clarifying and handling her feelings.

One last thought: If you are living a hectic life filled with many different inputs and stimulations, you are in danger of living an "undigested life." Writing in your journal at such times gives you a chance to go back over your day and extract meaning from a hurried meeting with a friend or retrieve the significance of some fleeting event.

Self-observation helps us to realize that we do not remember ourselves. What were those promises you made to yourself last week, two months ago? What were you feeling yesterday? What was your relationship with your mother a year ago? Do you remember how you got started on your current work or study?

Writing in your journal what you observe about yourself, all your self-promises, your decisions, and your aspirations can help you immensely in the task of "self-remembering."

Journals—or diaries—have been kept by numerous people who later achieved some fame (sometimes mainly by virtue of their diaries). I'm not suggesting that this should be *your* motive in keeping a journal, however.

The now-famous diaries of Anaïs Nin were begun by a little girl of eleven who had been moved to a new continent and a new culture and who wanted to maintain contact with her absent father, as well as to observe and comment upon her new surroundings. In her early years Nin used her diary to describe her feelings, to work out her conflicts, to record the poignant story of her miscarriage, to attempt to understand the relationship with her father.

When she was thirty-three, she wrote:

> Only you, my diary, know that it is here I show my fears, weaknesses, my complaints, my disillusions. I feel I cannot be weak outside because others depend on me. I rest my head here and weep . . . my diary seems to keep me whole.

A later description of her relationship with her diary implies some change:

> The diary was once a disease. I do not take it up for the same reason now. Before it was because I was lonely, or because I did not know how to communicate with others. I needed the communion. Now it is to write not for solace but for the pleasure of describing others, out of abundance.

After you have been keeping your journal for awhile, notice what seems to be its principal value for *you*.

CHAPTER 5

THE USES OF AUTOBIOGRAPHY

> Biography gives the melodic line of the life of a
> human being, heard against the contrapuntal
> background of social events.
>
> —MANAS

It may seem paradoxical that a gestalt therapist who empha-
sizes paying attention to present experience should suggest writing an autobiography as a growth-promoting procedure. Let me
defend my position.

Often a person who comes to see me is obsessed with her life
history . . . trying to remember it, to justify it, to bring some
meaning into it. One solution is to write your life's history in
detail, recalling the major events and relationships and your
feeling about them. Include the date on which you write this
autobiography, because a fascinating thing about autobiographies is that they change. The autobiography you write in 1980
will not read like the autobiography you wrote ten or twenty
years earlier. It's not just the addition of the subsequent years
that makes the difference. The events you chose to relate in
the early years can be different, the same relationships may
appear quite different in the two versions, and so on.

I still have a partial autobiography that I wrote in 1952. Comparing it with another written nearly twenty years later, you
would see that I chose different events to write about in the two
histories. Even when the same incident is discussed in both, the
"facts" are the same but the two interpretations are quite dis-
similar. In the first account I sound aggrieved, embittered, and

victimized by the circumstances of my childhood. In the second one the account is rounded out; you would read some understanding of where the "victimizing others" were, and see the strengths that I gained as a result of these events.

After you have finished writing your autobiography, let it sit for a few weeks. Then go back and reread it with the eyes of an Objective Observer. What is the feeling tone of this person's account of her life? Negative? Optimistic?

If it is heavily lopsided toward recall of the negative, deliberately set yourself the task of writing a new autobiography in which you record only the happy hours and the positive experiences. We gave this assignment to a group member in his mid-fifties who complained bitterly about how badly his stepmother had treated him. When asked to milk his memory for every nice time they had had together, he brought in a 16-page synopsis!

You can start your autobiography wherever you want to start. There are no rules. Those with a passion for order may wish to start with their earliest childhood memories and progress onwards. Or you might want to start with a major emotional event of your life. One of my university students began her autobiography with this sentence: "When I was 8, I was put on a train with a tag around my neck, told I was going to visit some very nice people, and I never saw my father again."

Fritz Perls wrote his autobiography, *In and Out the Garbage Pail*, in a totally subjective manner, choosing the topic for each day's meandering from what was "foreground" for him when he started the day's writing. Throughout the book he is keeping in touch with his awareness of the moment and sharing it with the reader. For instance:

> Topdog: Stop talking about Reich. Follow your intentions and stick to your theme, the oral resistances.
> Underdog: Shut up. I told you a few times, this is my book, my confessions, my ruminations, my need to clarify what is obscure to me.
> Topdog: Look! Your readers will see you as a senile, loquacious rambler.
> Underdog: So, we are back again to my *self* versus my *image*. If a reader wants to look over my shoulder, he is welcome, even invited to peep. What's more, I

have been prodded more than once to write my memoirs.

Topdog: Fritz, you are getting defensive.

You might want to write your autobiography in a similarly present-centered style. There are no rules.

There may be some time periods of your life that are blank for you. If so, you can be sure that they contain some important emotional material. You can help yourself to recover the "feel" of such a time by this regression-fantasy exercise. (It would be useful to have someone read this exercise to you, pausing at the dots. If that's not possible, you might tape-record it yourself and play the tape whenever you are ready to do this exercise.)

Age Regression Exercise

Get into a comfortable position.

Close your eyes.

Focus your attention on your breathing . . . chest rising . . . chest falling . . . chest rising . . . chest falling . . .

Now visualize a white screen in front of you. Project onto that screen a number, the same number as your present age . . .

Now see that number minus one year . . .
Now one year less . . .
One year less . . .
One year less . . .
One year less . . . (And so on until you arrive at the year desired. Let's take eight, as an example.)

Imagine yourself being eight years old again . . . Feel yourself in your eight-year-old body . . .

Now imagine that it's a schoolday and you're just waking up . . . Lying in your bed, what do you see in your room? . . . What smells do you smell? . . . What sounds do you hear? . . . Does anyone else sleep in this room? . . . Do you share your bed with anyone? . . .

Now feel yourself swinging your feet out of bed to get up. What does the floor or rug feel like? . . . What are you wearing? . . . Do you put on slippers or do you go barefooted? . . . What's the first thing you do when you get up? Go to the bathroom? Get dressed? Or what? What are your thoughts? . . .

Now feel yourself going to the bathroom. Where is it located in respect to your bedroom? Can you find your way there in the dark? See all the fixtures in the bathroom and feel yourself going through your usual morning routine . . .

Have you seen anyone yet? Talked to anyone? . . .

If you're not already dressed, feel yourself getting dressed. Do you choose your clothes? . . . or are they preselected for you? If you choose, how do you make your choice today and what do you choose to wear? . . .

Now see yourself going to breakfast. Where is breakfast? How do you get there? Is it fixed for you by someone else? Or do you fix it yourself? . . .

Do you eat alone? Or with others? . . . What are you eating? . . . How does it taste? . . .

Any conversation? . . . How do you feel about what's being said? . . .

Now see yourself getting ready to leave for school. Any special things happen here? . . .

Now start off for school. How do you get there? . . .
Walk? . . . Schoolbus? . . . Does your mother drive
you? . . . Do you ride your bike? . . .

Do you go alone or do you go with friends? Brothers?
Sisters? What happens on the way to school? How do
you feel about it? . . .

What's the weather like? Sunny? Rainy? Cloudy? Windy?
Cold? Warm? What month have you picked to relive
your eight-year-old experience?

Now see yourself arriving at school. Are you early? Late?
On time? If you're early, what do you do before time to
go in? What kids are you with? What are their names?
How do you feel about them? . . .

Feel yourself going into school. Which entrance did you
choose? What does it look like? How does it smell? What
sounds do you hear? . . .

Now take yourself through a typical day in school . . .
What classes do you have? What happens? What are
your teachers' names? How do you feel about them? . . .

Who are your best friends in your classes? . . . Who are
the kids you don't like? . . . See if you can focus on what
you don't like about them . . . Is there anyone you are
afraid of? . . .

Don't forget recess . . . what happens when you go out
to play? Who are you with? What kind of games do you
play? Or what do you do? . . .

And don't forget lunchtime. Do you go home for lunch?
. . . Or do you eat at school? . . . In the cafeteria? . . .
Or did you bring your lunch? . . . What happens when
you forget your lunch?

Be yourself eating lunch . . . Are you alone or are you with other people? . . . Where are you sitting? . . .

What are you eating? How does it taste? Smell? . . . What do others have to eat? How are you feeling? . . . What's happening? . . .

Do you play after you finish eating? Or how do you spend the time until class starts again? . . .

Now feel yourself finishing out the rest of the school-day . . .

Now it's time to go home . . . how do you get home? . . . Do you go straight home? Or do you go other places on the way? . . . Are you alone or with other people? . . . Stay in touch with what you're feeling and what you're doing . . .

Now you're home. What's the first thing you do when you get home? . . . And how do you feel about it? . . . Feel yourself spending the time however you spend it until time for supper . . .

Now it's suppertime . . . How does that appeal to you? . . . How many people at the table? Look at each of them . . . See how you feel about each one of them . . . What are you having for supper? How does it smell? Taste? Who cooked it? Who is serving it? . . . What's happening? . . . Who is talking? . . . Do you take part in the conversation? Or are you "quiet"? . . .

Now supper is over. What do you do after supper and before time to go to bed? . . . Feel yourself doing that. Do you have homework? . . . Chores to do? Can you watch television? . . . Listen to music? . . . Play? . . . Do you spend any time with your parents? . . . What is that time like for you? . . .

Now it's time to go to bed. How do you know it's "time to go to bed"? . . . Feel yourself going through your typical going-to-bed routine . . . Do your parents help you? . . . In what ways? . . . How do you feel about going to bed? . . .

Feel yourself lying in your bed. What is it like? Is it dark or do you have a light on? Is there anyone else in the room with you? Any toy that you take to bed with you? What things do you look at, what things do you touch, what sounds do you hear, what thoughts do you think as you lie there before you fall asleep? . . .

If you didn't do the whole exercise of a typical day, but allowed yourself to be "highjacked" by a particular memory of a specific day, that's fine. It's undoubtedly a memory that you need to deal with and make peace with. Be sure, however, that you now allow your Objective Observer to review that episode with you.

If you still have difficulty recalling the quality of your ninth year after the last exercise, then try this one:

House Plan Recall Exercise

Get a large sheet of paper and a ruler and draw a floor plan of the house where you lived when you were eight. Draw it as closely to scale as possible.

Start either with your bedroom or with the livingroom or with your typical entrance way.

Place the furniture within each of the rooms.

When you come to a room that you just "can't" remember, close your eyes and visualize the parts of it that you *do* remember. Then, almost like a blind person, feel your way from one wall to another, from one piece of furniture to another.

When you suddenly "out of the blue" remember a room, or a door, or a closet, or a certain dresser that you hadn't "remembered" for years, allow yourself to stay with it and to remember whatever associations that want to come forward at this time.

Another device to help break the logjam of a blocked memory period is to recall some object or scene that fascinated you. Close your eyes and visualize it in as much detail as possible . . . color, texture, sound, smell, taste . . . See what meaning it had for you and recall how your feelings and perception of the object or scene changed over time. Hermann Hesse describes his fascination with a "dancing idol from India" that stood in his grandfather's curio cabinet and the various interpretations he gave to it at different stages of his growth.

Perhaps you recall some special childhood game that you created in fantasy. Then allow yourself to be back in that space again, playing the game, spinning out the fantasy as you did then. One of my favorites was to play "Traffic" or "Life" on an intricately patterned oriental rug in the entrance hall of my childhood home. Certain paths I had designated as roads; others were sidewalks. Some patches of color were homes; others were stores, offices, and school. I dispatched two-inch-long cars called "Tootsietoys" on their various errands about the village, taking children to school or husbands to the train, hauling ice to the house or delivering milk. My favorite was a fresh fruit and vegetable wagon pulled by a horse that moved so slowly that the cars and even the bicycles would speed on past it. The grownups could never understand why I wanted to play with my Tootsietoys in the hall where there was a draft, rather than on the rug in some other, warmer room. I once tried to explain the geography of my village to one of them, but you know what poor imaginations grownups have and how hard it is for six-year-olds to help them to understand.

I never attempted to define for any of them the geography of the alternative landscape that my rug also served. On some days the paths were not roads but paths that twisted and turned —through forests, swamps, and meadows, and struggled up and down steep mountains. The Tootsietoys were no longer cars, but represented a variety of people, animals, goblins, and fairies, as some of the forests were enchanted and some of the mountains contained malevolent demons in their depths.

See where you are now as a result of this last anecdote. Are you caught up in remembering an invented game of your own? Or empathizing with my observation about unimaginative adults and recalling the chasm of communication? Or caught up with the content of my anecdote and focusing on me ("How old can she be?") rather than letting yourself associate back into your childhood?

Re-owning the Child Within

One bonus of doing your autobiography is learning to know, understand, love, and appreciate the child that you were. From observing many people in therapy I've concluded that until you can do this—love, cherish, understand and accept the child-that-you-were—your adult self will feel empty, tormented, lonely and deprived.

Nourishing the Child-That-You-Were Exercise

Chose a particularly traumatic period of your childhood.

See yourself as you were then, seated—or lying—or moving—in front of you.

Talk to the child-that-you-were.

Say any words of comfort or support that come to you.

Offer any advice.

Be the good parent (or fairy godmother) that you wish you had had.

Have a pillow represent the child-that-you-were and hold it, stroke, rock it.

When you finish this exercise, be sure to record your feelings and any insights that you garner. For most people this is a very moving experience and frequently a "break-through."

The basic purpose of writing autobiographical material is to help you to be done with the past, and to enable you to live in the present. If there is a particular episode that you keep returning to in your mind with feelings of anger or sadness or hurt or regret . . . "If I had only done this . . . said that . . . known more . . .", then you need to have a corrective emotional experience.

Corrective Emotional Experience Exercise

Write the event down like a short story in the present tense, told from your point of view. Try to remember what happened as accurately as you can. Reconstruct the dialogue. Record your feelings.

Then rewrite the story the way you would like for it to have happened. Confront your persecutor. Or revenge your tormentor.

Or love the person whom you neglected. Whatever you wish. Create new dialogue. Record your feelings. Invent your ending and resolution.

This can also be done out loud with a group of people. An ex-nun and I once convened a group of her friends for an evening to replay the court scene in which she had been expelled from the convent many years before. Her friends had either been at the convent at the time or were familiar with the religious life from other settings. We could have done it with people who had never been sisters. The only requirement would have been their good faith and a willingness to help in a reconstructive effort.

First we played it as it really happened. In this particular case it was useful to have people present who had actually been there, as they sparked memories for the protagonist that she might otherwise not have recovered.

Next we played the scene again as the leading lady wished it had been. She talked back to her accusers and startled herself with a speech in which she most articulately defended the moral principle on which she had acted. The end result was that this event was finished for her and she no longer finds herself "remembering" it.

Another use of autobiographical writing can be to tease out of the unconscious the meaning of some anniversary phenomenon. Lillian used to get depressed every April, regular as clockwork. So I had her relax, pay attention to her breathing for several cycles, and do this exercise:

Anniversary Exercise

"It's April 1979 and I'm living _____ and feeling _____" and so on. Then, after you develop the sense of your history for that year: "It's April 1978 and I'm living _____ and working _____" and so on for as far back as you can remember.

Lillian uncovered a history of several traumatic losses that had occurred in the Aprils of her early years (the death of her father, the forced giving-away of a pet dog). She also recalled some April losses in later years that she may have helped to happen by expecting them. "It's April, so what bad thing is going to happen *this* year?"—another example of a self-fulfilling prophecy.

If you have a special day that is typically anxiety-provoking or depressing for you, such as

Christmas
Thanksgiving
New Year's Eve
Your birthday
Passover
Labor Day
Friday the Thirteenth
Memorial Day
Hallowe'en
or whatever,

try this year-by-year recall and reconstruction of what you were doing and feeling, and the important events that were happening around you. Write them down. And see if some pattern emerges for you.

C.G. Jung was unquestionably one of the most erudite scholars of the last century or so. A list of his complete writings would take several dozen pages. Yet possibly the book of his that has influenced the greatest number of people is his simply written autobiography, the telling of his "personal myth," undertaken in his eighty-third year.

> My life story is a story of the self-realization of the unconscious . . . Recollection of the outward events of my life has largely faded or disappeared. But my encounters with the "other" reality, my bouts with the unconscious, are indelibly engraved upon my memory. In that realm there has always been wealth in abundance, and everything else has lost importance by comparison . . . I can understand myself only in the light of inner happenings. It is these that make up the singularity of my life, and with these my autobiography deals.

Like Jung, your autobiography may reflect the history and progression of your inner life with less attention paid to outside markings. Or you may be an extrovert, and your autobiography would then reflect a greater need to deal with the meaning of events outside yourself and your relationship to them.

Like Jung, you may want to write an autobiography toward the end of your life. A main psychological thrust in aging people . . . particularly if they have not worked on it before . . . is the search for the meaning of their lives. To have lived for no discernible purpose is demoralizing; the very common trait of elderly people of recounting their past experiences for any listener is, I believe, just this search for meaning and reassurance from youth that the old person's life was not a waste. As Einstein said, "The man who regards his life as meaningless is not merely unhappy but hardly fit for life." A group called the Gray Panthers has sponsored an oral history project where young people tape-record interviews with elderly people. "Old people, when they are asked by a young interviewer to recall their past and their achievements, begin to gain a new, positive respect for themselves. It is a very self-affirming experience for an old person to be asked by a young person what he or she has learned in life," states Maggie Kuhn, the group's founder.

Ulysses S. Grant, the victorious Union general who saved the Civil War for Lincoln, was swept into the presidency only to preside, however innocently, over a scandal-ridden administration. At sixty-two he had been defrauded by friends, was penniless and dying from throat cancer. Some other friends, among them Mark Twain, urged him to write his memoirs to recoup his fortunes and restore his good name. He hesitated, for he was no writer and he was very ill. But he undertook the project and in the last year of his life wrote his *Personal Memoirs*, achieving through them public respect and greatness again. He developed a new skill, that of writing, and in his writing discovered the meaning of his own life for himself before he died. He finished his manuscript only four days before his death.

It's possibly too crippling to experience each of our losses completely at the time they occur. So it seems a useful endeavor some time before death to re-encounter them and to evaluate in retrospect the apparent purposefulness of all those painful periods.

It can be similarly enriching to recount for yourself your times of glory and achievement.

The Glory-Brag Exercise. (This is best done in a small group where all share their experience at the end of the exercise.)

Take at least ten minutes to survey your life in solitude, eyes closed.

Review your life from your earliest childhood memory onwards.

Remember each achievement, each award, each thing you accomplished that you are proud of.

Eliminate any pejorative, undercutting remarks. (Example: "I was valedictorian of my high school class. Of course, there were only ten other people in the class." Knock out the second sentence, keep the first!)

Especially notice those events where your participation made a difference, where the outcome would have been different if you hadn't acted. (Examples: the time you spoke up and saved someone from losing a job, the time you were late for an appointment to help a lost child find his way home.)

And don't forget those events that you might discount because they are easy for others but were difficult for you. (Examples: the time you confronted a bully and were trembling as you did so; the time when unlinguistic you decided you'd raise your French grade from F to A and succeeded.)

Next, have each person take five minutes to share her memories with the rest of the group. The others are to stay alert for any slyly undercutting remarks.

This exercise could also be done alone. Write out a brief description of each of the glory-brag episodes. Then re-read what you've written after a cooling-off period. Be the Objective Observer and see if the writer is truly being proud or if there is some "modesty" or some deprecatory remarks slipping in.

CHAPTER 6

ON DREAMING

> God created the dreams to point out the way
> to the sleeper whose eyes are in darkness.
> —Ancient Egyptian text

Sigmund Freud said that dreams were the royal road to the unconscious. Fritz Perls called them the royal road to integration—meaning, a method of reclaiming previously disowned parts of the personality. Kilton Stewart described an uninterpreted dream as being "like an unopened letter from God." And according to Edgar Cayce, dreams are visions that can be crystallized. People have been fascinated with dreams and have regarded them as significant since ancient times. Remember how Joseph saved himself from a long term in jail and got himself established as Pharaoh's steward by his successful dream interpretations, first for the Pharaoh's butler and baker, and then for the Pharaoh himself?

With this long-standing historical interest in dreams, it's intriguing to me that the hard, scientific data on dreams came only in the last half of this century. In 1953, Aserinsky and Kleitman, working in the department of physiology at the University of Chicago, observed that sleeping subjects have periods of rapid eye movements (called REMs in the trade) and that these REM periods are associated with dreaming. Subsequent research, as reported by William C. Dement, established that everyone dreams (although not everyone remembers those dreams), that a typical adult will have four or five dream sequences per night (or 20 per cent of sleeping time), that people taking barbiturate sleeping pills, idiots, and senile people dream far less, and that premature babies spend up to 75 per cent of their sleep time in REM-sleep.

Dreaming is somehow essential to the organism. Subjects in a dream laboratory were awakened at the beginning of each REM period, allowed to go back to sleep, and always obtained their full baseline quota of sleep for the night. They were deprived only of their dreams. By the fifth night, when they were having 20 to 30 aborted REM periods per night, they had become tense, anxious, and irritable during the day and found it increasingly difficult to concentrate. A control group that was awakened as frequently during the night (but during non-REM or nondreaming periods) did not develop these symptoms. The experimental group's symptoms disappeared when they were permitted their normal sleep, and for the first few nights their REM periods were four times their normal frequency.

So the data are in and conclusive: We all dream and our dreaming provides some necessary function.

There are still still a few people, however, who swear that they don't dream because they have never recalled having a dream upon awakening. And many more recall their dreams so infrequently that they believe that they must dream less often than other people.

The data on dream recallers (i.e., people who recall at least one dream per month) compared to the nonrecallers are interesting. Goodenough and others found that the nonrecallers have more rapid REMs and make looking-away type of eye movements (almost as if they don't wish to see what's happening during the actual dream itself). They also tend to be more inhibited, more conformist, more self-controlled, and more apt to deny or avoid unpleasantness and confrontations in their daily lives than the dream recallers.

If you are a nonrecaller and want to join the ranks of the dream recallers, it's not too difficult . . . if you really *want* to remember them and agree to be in charge.

Setting the Intention to Remember your Dreams

Make a contract with yourself to write in your dream journal (or your regular journal) when you wake up.

Say to yourself just before you fall asleep: "The first thing I do when I wake up, I'm going to write down my dreams."

And do it. Have your journal by your bed, with pen inserted at the page where you wish to start writing. If you wear glasses, have them within easy reach also. When you awaken, write down whatever you recall. Even if it's only a fleeting impression or feeling. Even if it's only four words. "I'm in a meadow," for example. Resist the voice that says, "You didn't remember enough to be worth recording." That's a saboteur subpersonality speaking. Possibly the act of writing down, "I'm in a meadow," will elicit more details about the meadow and some action in the meadow. And even if those four words are all you get, don't berate your unconscious—thank it, and ask for a fuller recall next time.

Even if you have absolutely no recollection of a dream, sit up gently and start writing: "Alarm went off. I have no recollection of dreaming. I feel _____," or whatever. Something *will* emerge if you maintain this discipline.*

Until you are an experienced dream-recollector, I would advise you to set only the intention to remember your dreams. For if you also set the intention to remember to make a long distance call before 8, or to check to see if your teenage son is home, or to put out the garbage, you will likely wake up with the set to go into action on the second intention, and your dreams will quickly slip away.

You might also have a dialogue with your "absent" dreams.

---

*You could also use a tape recorder if that would be easier. Some people, however, find that the intellectual effort of figuring out which buttons to push wakes them up completely and the dream vanishes.

Dialogue with Absent Dream

First, as yourself, talk to the vanished dream. Tell it how you feel about its unavailability. Tell it what you want from it.

Then be the dream. Perhaps as the dream you will want to defend yourself, or to attack the dreamer, or to tell her how she avoids remembering you. (I don't want to write your scenario for you; let it develop with several back-and-forths.)

Or there's a third technique that I've used in workshops, and which you could use in your friendship circle.

Dream Invention

Invent a dream that each person in your group might have had. Then work on each of these "dreams" as if it were your own truly-dreamed dream.

Probably, however, most of you do remember a fair number of your dreams—possibly one a night, possibly one a week, maybe one a month—and are wondering what use can be made of them.

Along with Fritz Perls, I see the dream as an existential message from the dreamer to himself, a statement about who he is and what his life situation is like.

I would first suggest a very literal, common-sense approach to the dream. Frequently our dreams serve to remind us of the contents of the day, which we had noticed only subliminally, possibly due to the press of a large input of competing stimuli.

A dream of someone wearing platform shoes (before they were in style) helped me to realize that I hadn't been wanting to notice how self-important and grandiose that person (my then lover) was behaving. Dreams concerning foods or your body should first be examined quite literally as possible messages from your body to eat (or to avoid eating) these foods, or to examine or to take particular care of certain parts of your body. The psyche seems to know when a disease process is beginning, before it becomes manifest in actual somatic symptoms. So your dreams, properly interpreted, can be an early-warning system of possible future illness that can then be averted.

Your dreams can give you other kinds of warnings, too. I once had a dream concerning a young woman, whom I was seeing, who was afraid that her father would murder her. My dream went like this:

> She hides from him in my home. He finds her there, shoots her, and leaves. I pick her up, put her in my car, and race to UCLA Emergency. I try to blow my horn, it doesn't work, so I drive in erratic zig-zags to alert the other drivers and get through the traffic quickly. A policeman stops me. "Thank goodness, you've come," and I tell him the situation. He puts on his siren and precedes us through the traffic, clearing a path.

Obviously, there are many elements in this dream that bear working on: my relationship, therapeutic and otherwise, to the girl who gets shot, the would-be murderer, the policeman, also my need to be a heroine! However, the part that struck me most forcibly when I awoke was how frightening it had been to undertake that drive with no horn, and how foolish I had been to drive my BMW for over a month with a non-functioning horn. So that day I had the horn repaired. Now, I had known that my horn was not working. What I was ignoring was my anxiety at driving a car with no working horn, just because I felt that I was "too busy" to get it fixed.

A very dramatic example of a warning dream is given by Kathleen Jenks in the narrative of her personal growth through a Jungian-oriented self-analysis of her dreams. Early in the book she relates this dream, which she had one month after she first made love with Rob:

I was invited to a house filled with girls, plain-looking but pleasant. Each had once been Rob's lover —some went as far back as his high school years. Three were pregnant . . . It was appalling that he had had so many girls and had left them in such states . . . Then something very weird happened. They had to be sure they all had the "mark." They held up their hands and I was puzzled. I looked at them and was shown diagonal cuts across one or two of each girl's fingers . . . I said I didn't have this and one of them took my hand and looked at it closely. The cuts were there— very small and very slight. Then I remembered that he had scratched my hand one night . . .

Unfortunately, she chose to ignore the obvious message of the dream, and continued with her doomed infatuation with Rob.

The Metaphorical Meaning

If, however, you examine the dream for its literal message and find none, then it's time to approach the dream for its metaphorical meaning.

I see dream symbols not as an attempt to conceal or censor, as Freud claims, but as a picturesque shorthand used by the psyche. This shorthand is always idiosyncratic; there's no standard Gregg or Pitman translation. In fact, beware of therapists, friends, spouses, or dream experts who try to tell you what the symbols of your dream mean. By all means, listen to any interpretations; they might suggest a meaning that will ring true for you. But reject any proffered interpretation that doesn't resonate with you. Only you can decode your dreams.

Here are some suggestions to help you with your search for the cipher:

I. According to Fritz Perls, each part of the dream represents a part of the personality that has (possibly) been disowned. So take on the personality of each person, each object, each element in the dream.

Working on Your Dream

Be that person or object or element. Describe yourself. "Tell us your story," as Fritz Perls used to say.

What are you doing in the dream?
What are you feeling?
What are your relationships with the other dream figures and with the other objects in the dream?

What do you want?
Have dialogues with other parts of the dream.

It's useful to do this out loud. It's also useful to do it with an audience, a therapist or an objective friend who will feed back her perceptions of qualities that you might miss! The volume or quality of your voice, your posture, a twisting of the handkerchief, a tightening of your throat, a clenched fist, your general mood.

You can also do it silently. It's useful to write out the dialogue.

And as you enact each part, be alert for the emergence of associations to your current life. Or to the book, TV program,* or conversation right before bedtime that you didn't have time to process. You will usually experience an "ah-ha" sensation when the right fit is made.

How do you know where to start working on your dream or which elements to identify with? There are no rules. You can identify with each and every part of the dream. For instance, if I had wanted to work on my heroine dream in this metaphorical way I could have been the murderer, the young victim, the policeman, the heroine, the automobile, the emergency room of the hospital, and the non-functioning horn.

---

*Every morning during the week that *Roots* was screened on TV, I made at least one association to the episode of the night before. And I heard many *Roots*-related dreams from people that week. The effect of *Holocaust* was equally remarkable.

Be sure to include those parts of the dream that seemed most vivid, and where you felt the most emotion. Here's a checklist of parts of the dream with which you can identify:

A. Be the landscape or the environment, which could include a house, or the air, or the rain, or a desert, etc. Fritz once asked a man who had had a dream of riding a horse in Central Park to be the bridle path, and the man immediately replied, "What, and have all those horses shit on me?"

B. Be all of the people in the dream. If they are strangers, see if they remind you of anyone who is important in your life.

C. Be any object that links and joins, such as bridges, telephone lines, highways, and railroad tracks.

D. Be any unusual element, such as a safety lock that is on the *outside* of your car door, or a flying cat, or an object that mysteriously disappears only to reappear.

E. Be any interesting and mysterious object, such as a wrapped package, an unopened letter, or an unread book.

F. Be any powerful energy object, such as a tidal wave, or an automobile, or an electrical generator.

G. Be any religious objects from a crucifix to a statue of Buddha.

H. Be any object (or person) whose left side is different from its right side. Be the left side, then be its right side. Possibly have a dialog between the two.

I. Be any two contrasting objects, such as a new carpet and a worn carpet, or a young woman and an old woman.

J. Be anything in your dream that is missing. It could be something you have lost in your dream and for which you are actively searching. It could be a missing part of a signpost. Or a half-written word on a notepad. ("Promis" on a scrap of paper was the beginning of "promiscuous" in one man's dream.)

Sometimes there will be an important missing object in your dream that you don't realize is missing. This is where that therapist or objective friend can be useful again.

Lucy worked with me on a dream that had two segments: a woman being wheeled into surgery on a gurney and then the same woman waking up in the recovery room. I asked her to be the surgeon and reenact the missing scene between the two fragments. In doing this Lucy realized that the dream was about her recent hysterectomy and she did some much-needed grief work for her uterus (which was another missing part).

If someone has a dream that includes the Sun, Mercury, Venus, Mars, Jupiter, Saturn, Uranus, Neptune, and Pluto, he may need some outside help to make him realize that there is a planet missing from his solar system. Someone with his "head in the stars" may find it hard to see the obvious, which, of course, is Earth. It would be very useful and enlightening for such a person to identify with Earth for a change!

II. Be alert for any puns or colloquial expressions. These days a dream of a loaf of bread may be a dream about money. Or it may conjure up the need for "a jug of wine and thou" to be complete. It's your dream, so only your associations are valid. Ann Faraday has an excellent chapter in *The Dream Game* on the many puns she has collected from her subjects. A dream of her own contains two puns: A man in long white underpants shoots her down with a machine gun. The meaning of this dream occurred to her later that day when she was waiting to appear on a radio talk show with Long John Nebel and suddenly recalled some gossip about his hostile treatment of guests. She had repressed this information so her unconscious was sending her a warning that a man in "long johns" might try to "shoot her down."

III. Notice any numbers that appear in your dream (house number, number on a roulette wheel, someone's announced age, the price of an object, etc.) Explore your associations with those numbers.

IV. Notice how you are feeling when you wake up from your dream. This feeling-state—fear, joy, sadness, anger, frustration, puzzlement—may be your best clue as to the meaning of the dream.

V. Notice the colors in your dream. Any particular associations to these colors? You might want to draw certain parts of your dream. If there is a very special color in your dream, see if you can match the color exactly.

VI. My suggestion for finding the message of the dream (if it doesn't become apparent as you work on it as described above) is to have a dialogue with the dream. Ask the dream (or the Dream Sender within you, who sent you the dream) what message it has for you for your continuing growth. Then change places. Be the Dream Sender. Tell your Self what message you have to deliver.

If you emerge with a long, rambling statement, my hunch is that you are avoiding a shorter, pithier sentence that could be an inducement to action. I sometimes ask people to reduce their messages to a few words that could go on a poster, and then suggest that they make the posters and hang them on their walls at home. Here are some of their products:

Give yourself a CHANCE.
Give yourself the TIME.

The bough may break,
but the tree will stand.

Cross the river
where you are.

Don't tie your ship to a
single anchor (or pin your
life on a single hope).

VII. When you have finished your work on your dream, translate it into some kind of action that can be undertaken NOW. As in the work with fantasies, this is necessary to be grounded.

If your dream tells you to take some time for yourself, then plan precisely how you can cut back in your busy work schedule. If the Dream Sender urges you to cross the river now (instead of walking toward a possible "better bridge" downstream), then plan when and how to take the action to which the dream was metaphorically referring. If your dream is warning you not to tie your ship to a single anchor (and is really saying, don't let your accounting practice depend on one single large client), then realistically see what you can do to enlarge your clientele and then make those actual moves.

VIII. You might want to start a glossary of your own dream symbols and their very special and private meaning for you.

Nightmares

Nightmares are especially important dreams to work on. They are sometimes caused by two warring subpersonalities within you. When you discover the conflict and find some way to reconcile their diverse needs, there will be much energy released for whatever it is you need to do.

People frequently wake themselves up from a nightmare just before the ending. They are either perched like Pauline on the edge of a cliff, with the ground crumbling beneath them, or tied to a railroad track with an express train thundering toward them, or at the steering wheel of a car whose brakes have failed, careening down a steep hill, or . . . If this happens to you, try this gestalt technique: Finish the dream. Continue the action in your imagination.

Finishing an Interrupted Dream

Put yourself back into the dream.

Feel the same frightening feelings.

Continue the action.

Bring the dream to a genuine—not interrupted—ending.

One of the several unfortunate consequences of taking barbiturates to sleep (and becoming addicted to their use) is that when people cut back rapidly on their sleeping medication, they experience "REM sleep rebound," or a dramatic increase in the number of dream sequences per night. Some of these dreams may be terrifying nightmares.*

Senoi Dreamwork

If by any chance, *while* you are having the nightmare, you realize that you are dreaming, by all means continue the dream action. Don't say, "Oh, thank God, it's only a dream," and permit yourself to wake up. Confront your attacker—the robber, tidal wave, tiger, or whatever—and don't run away. He may capitulate when he sees your new show of strength or cleverness, and become a "paper tiger"! Or you may have to fight him to the death. If this latter is the case, know that you may call on your friends—or a fairy godmother—to help you. (After all, anything is possible in a dream.) Better yet, perhaps you can make him into an ally. It's important that you emerge unharmed. In the confrontation that you permit—knowing that nothing can harm you—you can learn some very valuable lessons.

---

*To prevent this, users of large amounts of sleeping pills should cut back at the rate of one therapeutic dose every week or ten days, with the goal of eliminating the pills and the pill-induced insomnia completely. Abrupt withdrawal, or the "cold turkey" method, can be quite dangerous. In addition to the severe nightmares, convulsive seizures are a possibility.

This is a dream technique that was developed by the Senoi, a tribe in Malaysia noted for its cooperative philosophy of living and virtual absence of "mental disease."* Their dream life is taken very seriously. At breakfast each day, the children are encouraged by the elders of the tribe to tell their dreams. They are then instructed how they can confront their demon-attackers the next night, and that they must always advance and never retreat, calling on dream images of their friends for help if necessary.

The tribe believes that a person who does not conquer the evil spirit in his dream and who does not convert this spirit into his ally will be forever in the power of the demon. And, further, this demon will be joined by other evil spirits who will continue to assail the dreamer with increased strength. If he continues to avoid confrontation with them in his dreams, they will be augmented by still more hostile spirits until he is facing overwhelming odds.

If a child has a dream of falling and wakes up frightened before the fall is finished, he is told to relax and enjoy himself the next time he falls in a dream. "The falling spirits love you. They are attracting you to their land." In this new land the child is exhorted to discover and bring back something of beauty or use to the tribe. It might be a new dance, some new music, a tool, or useful knowledge. Through this educational process, the dream that starts out as an anxiety dream of falling is transmuted to a joyous one of flying, and creative discoveries for the benefit of the total group become a possible and valued accomplishment.

Repetitive Dreams

If you dream the same dream or a similar dream repeatedly, this is a sign that the dream contains some important unfinished business. Once you learn to understand the dream, then its recurrence can alert you to whatever is triggering the dream in your current life.

Let me describe a recurrent dream that I had for about thirty-five years. It began when I was fourteen and started high school.

---

* The tribe was first studied by Kilton Stewart in the 1930s.

Unlike junior high school, we now had a different class in a different room each period. And unlike any normal high school, our schedule changed each day, so that if Monday I had French first period, English second period, Geometry third period, and History last period, on Tuesday it would be English, Geometry, two others, History and French. Wednesday, the schedule would be Geometry, two others, History, French, and English. Confusing! So we had our weekly schedules written in the front of our notebooks and pasted in our lockers. In my original dream . . .

> I can't get my locker open, my notebooks are all inside the locker, and I can't remember what class I'm supposed to be going to. I wake up in a panic.

From a simple anxiety dream prompted by the stressful situation of a new and confusing school, the dream got more elaborate through the years. I might be in college and suddenly remember at the end of the semester that I had registered for some esoteric course on Horace or Molière (courses that in real life I had never even considered taking). I've got to find someone in the class and quickly ascertain what material has been covered so I can cram for the final exam. The dream would be a clear signal that in my waking life I was venturing into a new and confusing territory, possibly taking on too much, and was definitely afraid of failing.

Peggy had a recurrent dream:

> I am straightening up a livingroom, dusting, putting things away. Then through an archway I see a young couple lounging on a bed in the next room. They look as if they would like to make love, and their eyes seem to tell me to turn out the light and go away. I pretend not to see them and very deliberately continue to fuss around in the livingroom. I wake up feeling very sad and lonely.

When I had her dialogue with the young couple, they quickly became her parents. It emerged that Peggy had slept in a bed in a corner of their bedroom until she was ten years old. Until she worked on her dream, she had never dealt with her feelings about witnessing her parents' lovemaking or her power (by fussing around about going to sleep) to thwart their pleasure together.

Lucid Dreams*

A lucid dream is a dream in which the dreamer is aware that he is dreaming. He has access to the memories of his waking life and can evaluate situations and make decisions based on such information. Many people have been deliberately developing this ability to dream with awareness and are finding, as did the Senoi, that when you master a situation in the dream world, you achieve equivalent mastery in the waking world.

As an example: I haven't had my high-school-locker type of dream for several years now. In the final version—

> I have two days to find my classroom and my class-mates before finals. Otherwise I will get an F on my record. I go to the registrar's office to try to locate the classroom, but it is closed . . . locked! At this point I realize I am dreaming, and the whole situation becomes hilarious. I think, let them give me an F. I've got a Ph.D. and don't need to bother about grades and records any more, and I'd much rather go to the beach than study for some stupid final in French liter-ature. And so I go to the beach and body-surf and then meet some friends and we eat supper around a campfire and have a great and joyous time.

Since that dream, the world's concepts of "success" and "fail-ure" have been quite irrelevant for me, in contrast to earlier years. That subpersonality who was so concerned with "what will people think" no longer bothers me.

Learning to be conscious during your dream life seems to me to be part of a program of becoming totally conscious and being self-observant at all times. I imagine that the truly liberated per-son would be someone who has achieved this goal of total con-sciousness, and his thoughts while asleep would be as accessible to him as his thoughts while awake.

The Dream Sender

In addition to learning to remember your dreams, you can also learn to dream specific dreams on demand. If, for instance, you failed to get the message from a dream, you can ask the Dream Sender to give you a dream that will explain the first

---

*A term coined by Frederick Van Eeden to describe hundreds of such dreams he experienced and recorded between 1898 and 1912.

dream. Just as in remembering your dreams, it is necessary to set the intention:

Asking for a Certain Dream

Say to yourself just before you fall asleep, "My dreams tonight will explain last night's dream. And the first thing I'll do when I wake up is to write down those dreams."

You can also ask the Dream Sender to let you re-dream a certain significant or satisfying dream.

A very important use of your Dream Sender is to ask for a dream that will give you an answer to a specific question or help in making a certain decision. A couple of years ago I had a very bad cold while I was staying at a temporary home in Germany. I was to leave the next morning to do a workshop in Poland, a twenty-four-hour train trip away. I had vacillated in my decision-making about whether I should cancel the trip and the workshop. When I went to sleep that night, I asked for a dream that would tell me whether I should go or stay. I woke up in the middle of the night with a hideous attack of coughing and dashed for the bathroom a long hall away. As I was sitting on the toilet I remembered I had intended to have a definitive dream. At first I felt I had lost it, then I remembered something about being in a group of people and speaking German. My Critic subpersonality got very annoyed at this point. Not only was this not my definitive answer dream, but also it sounded like one of what I call my "show-off" dreams. So I angrily said to myself, "Jan, you know you don't speak German. If you were really speaking German in that dream, I'd like to hear you re-produce just one sentence of dialogue." And then the one word "bleiben" popped into my head. I knew I had heard the word, but I couldn't think what it meant. I was on my way to look it up in the dictionary when I remembered the situation in which I had heard it, and realized it meant "to stay." This was too powerful a message for even the most adamant stage-trooper to ignore, so I cancelled the workshop and stayed in Germany. And fortunately so, because the next few days I was far too sick to be traveling or working.

Your Dream Sender is a very creative person and can be helpful to you in your waking life in a variety of ways. There are innumerable inventions and artistic creations that were initiated by dreams. Elias Howe had begun to despair of designing a sewing machine that would work until in a dream he saw his sewing machine needle with the eye at the *bottom*, rather than in the middle or at the top—as in his models that wouldn't sew properly.

August Kekulé had been wrestling with the problem of how to conceptualize the benzene molecule. There weren't enough hydrogen atoms to satisfy the valence of the six carbon atoms when they were placed in a straight line (which is how organic compounds had been arranged up until this time). He fell asleep. "The atoms flitted before my eyes . . . wriggling and turning like snakes . . . One of the snakes seized its own tail and the image whirled scornfully before my eyes. As though from a flash of lightning I awoke: I occupied the rest of the night in working out the consequences of the hypothesis. Let us learn to dream . . ." And this is how Kekulé conceived of arranging the atoms of the benzene molecule in a ring, a discovery that was the foundation of the chemistry of dyes and pharmaceutical compounds.

Raymond de Becker reports many other instances of dream-inspired creativity. Niels Bohr conceived the model of the atom from a dream about the planets revolving around the sun. Dante's *Divine Comedy*, Goethe's *Faust, Part II*, and Coleridge's *Kubla Khan* were inspired by dreams. And the works of Mozart, Schumann, Wagner, Tolstoy, de Quincey, Poe, Saint-Saëns, Van Gogh, Heine, Voltaire, and La Fontaine were influenced by their dreams.

Otto Loewi received the Nobel prize for a discovery that was the result of a double dream. He had been puzzling about how the nervous system affects the heart beat. During a dream he "discovered" the principle of chemical action on the nervous system and designed the experiment that would demonstrate it. He scribbled some notes and went back to sleep. However, tragedy! Next morning he couldn't decipher his notes. The following night he slept very fitfully, but in the middle of the night he redreamed his solution. This time he didn't take a chance on writing notes, but went straight to his laboratory to start the experiment.

I discovered this ability to ask the Dream Sender for a definitive answer dream when I was about thirteen, possibly because I had so many adult responsibilities at that time and needed some seemingly "outside" and grown-up advice. So I was quite surprised some years later to learn that the deliberately induced dream was an ancient and respected practice in many cultures, such as those of Greece, Rome, Egypt, China, Iran, and India.

From the Sixth Century B.C. to the Sixth Century A.D., the Greeks and Romans practiced *dream incubation*, or going to a sacred place in order to receive a useful dream from a god. The dreamer might ask for divine instructions for a problem in masonry, or a remedy for sterility, or for a diagnosis and cure of other ailments. He would go to one of the several hundred temples of Aesculapius; there he would chant with the priests, abstain from wine, sexual intercourse, and certain foods that were believed to hinder dream production, and do some ritual bathing for purification. Then, after having been invited in a first dream by the god, he would spend the night in the *abaton*, lying on the bloody skins of the recently sacrificed sheep and oxen with only the writhing (though harmless), sacred snakes of the temple for company. With all this preparation and expectation it's not surprising that he would have a significant dream. Evidently many healings took place. Stelae found at Epidaurus describe the diseases of seventy patients and the dreams that cured them. If, however, the pilgrim had an obscure dream, he could go to one of the local entrepreneurs in dream interpretation. At Memphis, the plaque over one such shopkeeper's door read: "I interpret dreams, having the god's mandate to do so."

A contemporary psychologist has revived the incubation ritual. Just as the temples accepted only those people whom the god had first advised in a prior dream, so also Henry Reed waits for people to seek him out rather than asking for volunteers.

The Islamic people continue the practice of the induced dream, but not in temples. They call it "istiqâra." A person with a difficult problem recites a special prayer recommended by Mohammed and then goes to sleep expecting to receive the answer or solution in his dream. This is done by the traveler on the eve of a trip, the author before writing, or the statesman before an important policy decision. It is alleged that Dr. Mossadegh, the prime minister of Iran, decided to nationalize the Anglo-Iranian Oil Company as a result of such an induced dream in 1950. A shining apparition said to him, "This is not the time to rest, arise and break the chains of the people of Iran."

Individuation Dreams and Their Symbols

Individuation is Jung's word to describe the process by which you become the definite and unique being that you in fact are. There are two growth processes needed to accomplish it.

First you must rid yourself of the false wrappings of the *persona*, which is Jung's term for your facade, social roles, and games. Many of the exercises and suggestions given so far in this book—journal writing, the Evening Review, subpersonalities, disidentification exercise, self-observation, and gestalt dreamwork in particular—should help you to discern your *self* (who you really are) as distinct from the social roles that you play in the world.

You need also to come to terms with the primordial images (or archetypes) of the *collective unconscious* so that they will no longer be able to influence your behavior. These are myths and symbols that, according to Jung, seem to be universal for all people in all cultures and in all historical periods. Unlike the personal unconscious, whose contents were originally conscious but then were forgotten or repressed, the contents of the collective unconscious have never been conscious and were not personally acquired, but are a racial inheritance. Examples of such archetypes are the eternal child, the witch, the mother, the hero, and so on. It could be a mythological figure of which the dreamer has no conscious knowledge. For instance, a woman came to the first meeting of one of my dream classes with a dream in which there was a teacher named Minerva. The student disclaimed any knowledge of mythology, yet further work on the dream demonstrated that she expected me to be very wise.

Jungian analysts believe that some people (especially people in the second half of their lives) have dreams that demonstrate this process of individuation. The beginning of the process will be heralded by dreams containing floods, earthquakes, holocausts, or similar symbols of psychic transformation.

Next will occur dreams about the *shadow* or the dark side of humanity and himself that the dreamer has rejected, condemned, or ignored. In dreams, these rejected characteristics are projected on another person, frequently a "black man." Jung felt that it is essential for all of us to re-own this universal shadow. According to his biographer, Laurens van der Post, he believed:

> The individual who withdraws his shadow from his neighbour and finds it in himself and is reconciled to it as to an estranged brother is doing a task of great universal importance.

The persecution of the Jews by the Nazis and of Blacks by Whites are two hideous examples of the shadow unchecked and permitted expression on a national level.

The concept of the shadow is not a Twentieth Century or even a Nineteenth Century discovery. Plato wrote in *The Republic:* "Even in the most respectable of us there is a terribly bestial and immoral type of desire, which manifests itself particularly in dreams."

To work on your own shadow, be sure to identify, gestalt-style, with every sinister figure in your dreams. (You created this person in your dream. And every evil deed that he performs there is of your invention.) If you don't own this evil as part of your psyche, but continue to self-righteously condemn it in others, a sad and strange transformation occurs. *We tend to become what we condemn and oppose.* I suspect this is the meaning behind the New Testament injunction to "resist not evil." One of the tragedies of our history is that so often groups who wish to promote social justice conceptualize the group in power as the enemy and evil. By the time they have succeeded in overthrowing the "enemy" they have acquired all of his characteristics.

The shadow can also be a friend whom you secretly despise or envy. And it will be your flip side. If you are sexually liberated, your shadow may be someone whom you perceive as "prudish." If you are a jet-setter, expect a prosaic stay-at-home clerk-typist. Or if you maintain voluntarily a 60-hour work week, your shadow may present itself as a "bum" waiting in line for his unemployment check!

Men can expect to have dreams of their *anima* and women of their *animus*, which according to Jung are the archetypes of their unconscious and unexpressed feminine and masculine parts. Anima examples are the mysterious unknown woman, Dante's Beatrice or Liv Ullmann or Barbra Streisand. Animus examples are the dashing Arab, the mysterious stranger, the knight in shining armor, Robert Redford or Paul Newman, or frequently a group of men.

See what your anima or animus is doing in your dream. Imagine doing that activity yourself. We cannot be whole until we have reclaimed the opposite-sex side of ourselves. The man needs to reown his gentle, nurturing, artistic side, rather than projecting it onto his anima (whom he may pursue fruitlessly in his waking life). The woman needs to reown her aggressive, logical, thinking abilities, rather than always casting these onto her animus and onto the men in her life.

As the individuation process moves along, there may be dreams containing progress symbols such as voyages, highways, forks in the road, or wading across a stream from one bank to another.

Some archetypes that are sure to emerge in dreams are those of the "wise old man" and the "wise old woman." They symbolize that you are about to withdraw your projection of wisdom from your outside mentor—Plato, Christ, Swami Muktananda, your dissertation chairman, Einstein, Bertrand Russell, or whomever—and give it to the guru within.

Finally, you can anticipate having some dreams that seem to denote pure energy or the unity of all life. I'd rather not suggest illustrative examples here, but let you dream your own.

If this section on individuation dreams has caught your interest, I'd like to suggest that you do some reading about myths and symbols. At the end of the chapter is a reading list that will help you to fathom the force and usefulness of individuation dreams.

Mandala Dreams

A mandala is a perfectly balanced design whose center is particularly important. They are typically circular but they can also be square. They are frequently used in the East, especially Tibet, as objects for contemplation. The design is constructed to encourage the viewer to focus on the center and to ignore the outer designs.

Jung was very intrigued with mandalas and studied them in many cultures. He found that his patients often had mandala dreams at that point in time when the Self emerges as the center of the integrated psyche and also at times of psychic dissociation and disorientation when some "self-healing" is needed.

Here's an example of a mandala dream:

> I'm walking in the woods when I come to a very large cleared area that is square in shape, with four very tall pine trees marking each of the corners. As I move into the cleared area I step over a large, long log that is lying across my path. I notice that it is joined by two other logs which are joined by two other logs which all together form a pentagon. In the center of this pentagon is a small circle of dark rocks, some of which are carved in interesting shapes. Then I see that these rocks must have once contained a campfire. I go over to examine the area to see if there are still any live embers. I hear a roar behind me and realize that the forest is on fire. I look around and see a circle of red and yellow flames leaping above all but the highest four trees. I know that I must stay in the safety of the pentagon and the rock circle until the fire has burned itself out.

List of Suggested Readings on Myths and Symbols

1. Raymond de Becker, "A Kaleidoscope of Dream Images," in *The Understanding of Dreams and Their Influence on the History of Man.* London: Allen Unwin, 1968, pp. 301–346.

2. Manly P. Hall, *Studies in Dream Symbolism.* Los Angeles: Philosophical Research Society, 1965.

3. C.G. Jung, *Man and His Symbols.* New York: Doubleday, 1964.

4. Joseph Campbell, *The Hero with a Thousand Faces.* Cleveland: World Publishing, 1956.

5. Joseph Campbell, *The Mythic Image.* Princeton: Princeton University Press, 1974.

6. Edith Hamilton, *Mythology.* New York: New American Library, 1940.

7. Maria Leach, editor, *Funk and Wagnalls Standard Dictionary of Folk Mythology and Legend.* Conklin, N.Y.: Crowell, 1972.

8. Alan Watts, *The Two Hands of God.* New York. Macmillan, 1969.

9. Edward Edinger, *Ego and Archetype.* New York: Penguin, 1972.

10. Frieda Fordham, *An Introduction to Jung's Psychology.* New York: Penguin, 1966.

11. J.E. Cirlot, *The Dictionary of Symbols.* New York: Philosophical Library, 1967.

CHAPTER 7

MEDITATION: WHAT, WHY, WHEN, AND HOW

> Meditation is first an effort, then a habit, and finally a joyous necessity.
>
> —Christmas Humphreys

> It's like coming home.
>
> —Lawrence LeShan

Earlier I mentioned that we would examine four tools that would be helpful in learning the art of self-observation: the journal, the autobiography, dreams, and meditation. Of these four, meditation is ultimately the most powerful tool, although also the most subtle.

What is meditation? Among other things, it is a discipline that enables you to take responsibility for the contents of your awareness; hence its inclusion in a book on learning to take charge of your thoughts. It's a method for creating a center of quiet and stillness within yourself. There you can become a detached observer of the stream of changing feelings, thoughts, and urges within you. Gradually you will understand their meanings and their beginnings.

The word "meditation" comes from the Latin "meditari," a passive verb that means "being moved to the center." This is what seems to happen after you have been meditating for awhile. Without willing or trying, you are moved to your center. That is, you have the sensation of being at a belvedere point from which you can see clearly, discriminate, set your priorities, be unperturbed in a crisis situation, and so on. From this place you can discover much about your *self-image*, or the person that you have thought you were. You will start to understand that person's script, his romantic story line. Was he neglected by his parents? If so, did he let this affect his life? Did her mother prefer her older sister? If so, is she still battling her sister to be Number One with mother? Is he someone who is afraid that life is passing him by? And so on. It will seem like the scenario for another person, and you notice that the old emotional "hurts" drop away.

Why do people meditate? Historically, the reason was undoubtedly spiritual or religious. Recently, however, people have been turning to meditation for stress reduction, or for a tool to help deal with obsessive thoughts.

Simons Roof says that the best definition of meditation is the act itself. I'm inclined to agree, so let's get on to the "how" of meditation.

First of all, there are many, many different techniques. I can't emphasize enough that there is no one "right" technique; all of the methods have value. I'm going to describe several different methods; I hope you will intuitively select one and then work with it for awhile—a minimum of three or four weeks—and see what happens.

It's best to meditate once a day at some regular time, ideally early in the morning before you start your daily routine. Plan to meditate from fifteen minutes to an hour. Fifteen minutes every day will yield more progress than one hour twice a week. But again there is no "right" length for your meditation. As you become accustomed to meditating, you will know when you're finished, whether it's after ten minutes or forty.

Next select your place. Some experts get very fancy here and suggest that you have a place set aside for meditation where no one else may enter, and that you wear special clothes and burn incense, and so on. I suspect that part of the value of those instructions is to ensure that you take your meditation seriously. This doesn't seem necessary to me (I know many people who bought special clothes for jogging or deep-sea diving, only to give up the sport after a few trials).

Do, however, select a place where you will not be disturbed. Hang a "Do Not Disturb" sign on the door, take the phone off the hook, or do whatever is needed in your particular situation.

Sometimes just getting up a half hour earlier than the rest of the family is all that's needed.

Now about posture: The Indians prefer the double-lotus position, and the Japanese squat on their buttocks. These positions work fine for them; their bodies learned such postures in childhood. The average Westerner over thirty will find these positions difficult to assume and the physical pain could be a distraction and a hindrance to meditation. You can meditate just as successfully sitting in a chair, so don't let anyone brainwash you into an uncomfortable imitation of another culture.

Wherever you sit, do sit with your spine erect. Not straight, because you have a natural curve to your spine. But not slumped. Center your body as you sit, make it comfortable. Feet on the floor. Hands placed lightly in your lap, or, if you prefer, with thumbs and index fingers touching, as many people of the East do.

All of the methods to be described have common qualities:

(1) They are designed to foster your concentration, which is the first stage of meditation. Have you ever seen a dog pointing at a rabbit or a cat watching a bird? You will develop that quality of one-pointedness as you learn to meditate. With the skill of one-pointedness, you will notice all sorts of secondary gains in your ongoing life: an ability to discriminate quickly the important from the nonimportant, greater efficiency in accomplishing both mundane and difficult tasks, less reaction in stressful situations, lowered heart rate, lowered blood pressure, and so on.

(2) They are simple, nothing terribly complicated.

(3) They are repetitive. It is the repetition that helps you to develop concentration, to deal with feelings of boredom, and to deal with all the various thoughts and resistances that will occur to you. Ram Dass gives an amusing account of the resistant thoughts he entertained during a ten-day course of all-day meditation: all the people he had ever known, all the best restaurants, all the places he still wanted to visit, all his theoretical models of what he thought was happening.

It's important to learn to observe these distracting thoughts in a calm, loving, dispassionate, and detached way. Eventually you will become the loving and impartial Witness of your inner process.

So to start your meditating:

1. Seat yourself.

2. Get your body comfortable with your spine erect.

3. Give yourself the intention to set aside your emotions and your "problems" for this period of time.

4. Close your eyes.

5. Set aside your judgments, expectations, fantasies of what your meditation experience will be. Allow the experience to happen. Set aside your competitive subpersonality who wants to learn to meditate more quickly and become more spiritual than your friends and colleagues!

6. Relax the muscles of your face and jaw. (Some people then produce a half-smile like that seen on statues of the Buddha or pictures of the Madonna.)

7. Regulate your breath. Breathing *through both nostrils*, count the number of units required for your incoming breath. Then allow the same count for your outgoing breath. Let your belly push out with your incoming breath, and then let your chest rise. Hold yourself motionless for an instant or two before letting the breath start to leave. Let your breath be gentle and inaudible. Then when you feel your breathing to be even, start your meditation technique.

1. *Contemplation of an Object*

Choose an object. It could be a seashell, a bowl of water, a twig, a rock, a tree, the flame of a candle, a heap of sand, a matchbox, a cactus, or whatever.

Concentrate all your attention on your object. *Look* at it with complete absorption, as if you had never seen such a thing before. Then close your eyes and touch it, if that's appropriate. Then back to looking, really looking. Each time you notice your attention going elsewhere, label the diversion and bring your mind kindly back to the object. "Whoops, I'm thinking about what I'm going to do when I finish meditating. Back to you, cactus. Your spines are not the same length," etc. And don't be hard on yourself for your wandering mind. Larry LeShan suggests that you treat yourself as a much-loved child whose parents want to keep you on the narrow sidewalk, despite the fascinating distractions of flowers, grass, and trees on either side. Don't stare, just look. If you find yourself staring, deliberately soften your eyes. And notice whether you still have your half-smile. After a while you will find yourself almost entering into the life of that object, merging consciousness with it.

2. Breath Counting

Taking full and even breaths, count them. "Breathing, one. Breathing, two," etc. You note "breathing" to yourself on the incoming breath and note the count on the outgoing breath. In one method you count sequentially. However, this can be distracting if you are striving to reach the goal of a certain number. Fixation on a future goal is counterproductive to a present experience of meditation. It's probably better to count to a certain number, either five or ten (ten is the number the Zen masters use), and then start over again at one.

Again, if you find yourself thinking of anything other than your count, gently remind yourself of your task and come back to the counting.

3. Breath Mindfulness

You observe, describe, and label your breathing. "I am breathing in a long breath. My abdomen is rising, now my chest. Now there's a gap. Now the breath is leaving," etc. In this technique you do not attempt to change your breathing, you just notice how it is. Go with the flow. Particularly notice the gaps between the breaths, the one between the incoming and outgoing and the other between the outgoing and the incoming breaths. At these times you are most in your center. Buddha supposedly said that if you can be aware of your breath for a single hour, you will be enlightened. (That means without losing awareness of even one breath!)

When a thought comes in, don't fight it, just acknowledge it, give it a label, and metaphorically put it on the shelf where you can find it again (if you want to) after your meditation.

Some thoughts will be very enticing, but you don't have to fall for the bait. You're in charge! If, however, you get some stupendous insight or the long-sought-for answer to a research problem, you might want to end your meditation to preserve the new thought. Most of these enticing thoughts will not be that profound!

4. *What's Going On at My Nostrils?*

Very simply, notice the air going in and out at the point where it enters or leaves your nostrils. *Don't* notice the gaps between breaths or whether your tummy is pushing out. That's not part of this exercise, much as your bored mind might like to try to enlarge the scope. It's as if you're noticing people going through a revolving door: "Here's one coming in, here's another going out." You don't pay any attention to where the breath goes when it enters the body or what happens to it when it leaves. Just keep your attention focused at the tip of your nostrils and notice what's happening there. Again, when a thought comes in, acknowledge it and put it aside.

In another version of this method you notice the incoming and outgoing breath at the level of the chest. You say to yourself, "Chest rising, chest falling."

5. *Mindfulness Meditation*

In this method you simply observe whatever happens. Label it and leave it. Any thoughts that occur. Any sounds you hear. And any thoughts that you think about those sounds. Your breathing. Any body sensations, an itch or a twitch. And your breathing.

If you find yourself constantly elaborating on thoughts, rather than labeling them and returning to the neutral, alert, and watchful center, remember to observe your breathing, because it's happening all the time. You may need to combine this technique with the breath-mindfulness technique.

When emotions or memories of painful experiences occur, don't allow yourself to become highjacked by them. Give them short process labels such as "sad feeling," "remembering," "angry feeling," "remembering, remembering." These memories and feelings will gradually decrease. More importantly, you will begin to identify yourself as the Objective Observer or Witness and not as the person who is disturbed by these thoughts and feelings. Properly carried out, this can be an important sanity-restoring exercise at times when you are feeling very "disturbed." You can practice mindfulness while doing any activity, for instance, while doing the dishes as described earlier.

6. A Few Hours of Mindfulness

Set aside a few hours when you can be alone. Do only simple work such as housecleaning, gardening, cooking, washing clothes, "straightening up." Work slowly (one-half your normal speed or less) with complete awareness of each part of each task. "Now I am scraping the carrot, now I am rinsing it, now I'm turning off the water, now I'm thinking about the drought in the Sahara, now I'm chopping the carrot, etc." acknowledging any extraneous thoughts that occur.

You might take a slow-motion bath, attending to each awareness. Or take a walk with complete mindfulness. Try eating a meal mindfully in slow motion. And faithfully acknowledge each thought that enters. This is a most powerful tool for learning the art of self observation.

7. Meditation with a Mantra

A mantra is a spiritually charged Sanskrit word or phrase such as *Om* or *Om Mani Padme Hum*, which is repeated over and over with the rhythm of your breath. (One repetition with your exhalation; a silent repetition with your inhalation.) These mantras were supposedly "received from the cosmos" centuries ago by revered sages and are said to carry vibrations that permeate and purify the mind and the body. English phrases can be used as a mantra, also the name of God in any language (*Hare Rama* or *Jehovah Elohim*, for example).

You can either chant your phrase out loud or say it to yourself inaudibly. Stay with the rhythm of your mantra and, as in the other meditative techniques, note any extraneous thoughts and awarenesses. Gently dismiss them and return to your task.

Mantra repetition is a useful meditative practice for beginners and especially for people with unusually busy "monkey minds." It will help you to clear your mind and be able to adopt the Witness or Objective Observer position. You will experience all the much-touted relaxation and physiological benefits—less reaction to stress, lowered heartbeat, lowered blood pressure, slower respiration, relief of migraine headaches and backaches—just as with the other meditative techniques that we've discussed. But at some point the mantra may become a hindrance to any further progress in meditation as you will have become addicted to it, or attached, as the Buddhists would say. If so, you may want to thank your mantra for all the help that it has given you, jettison it, and go on to another method of meditation.

There is a well-advertised meditation group that will sell you a supposedly personalized and unique mantra, but that's really quite unnecessary and rather costly ($200 for a working adult, at the time of this writing). Mantras are freely given by recognized teachers, and there is no need to pay for this privilege. Nor does it seem reasonable that a secret mantra intoned by you alone would be more powerful than a well-known ancient one used by millions of people.

8. The Who-Am-I? Meditation

I think you will be more successful with this meditative technique after you have had some practice with any of the first seven.

First do the Disidentification Exercise. (Chapter 2.) Then start asking yourself, "Who am I?" Don't rush the answers; think carefully. After you generate some answers, then ask, "Who is it that is answering?"

Watch your mind as it thinks through the question. Then ask, "Who is this thinker?" Each answer should generate another question. If the answer is, "I am a school teacher," then realize "A school teacher is an occupation. Who is the I who teaches school?" If the answer is, "Someone who loves children," then realize, "That is an adjective, an attribute. Who is the person who has this feeling for children?" And so on and on. Who is the I that is happy today and was sad yesterday? Angry an hour ago and loving now? Who is the I who observes these changing moods? Who is the I who dreams when the body sleeps? Who is the I who says, "I have a body, but I am not my body?" Who is the I who says, "I don't know!" If this type of meditation interests you, you might want to read what Ramana Maharshi has to say about self-inquiry.

Detours, Dangers, and Delusions on the Path of Meditation

Allowing yourself to be booby-trapped and side-tracked by having visions, seeing bright lights, or having "powers." These are frequent byproducts of sustained meditation, but not the main goal. Pursuing them can be a dangerous detour.

Bragging to others about these states. You can know that those people who buttonhole you with "Monday I had the highest experience I've ever had and blah-blah-blah" are deluding themselves about their meditative progress, in addition to being the biggest bores on the block.

Becoming rigid. Believing that there is only one "right" way to meditate. (Each person has to feel her way to the practice or practices best suited to her needs.) Ridiculing those who don't choose *your* path.

Expecting miraculous changes instantaneously. The changes are slow and subtle, and your friends will probably comment on them before you notice them.

Switching brands, trying to sample the whole smorgasbord of meditative techniques too rapidly. Stay three weeks to a month with any practice that you start.

Neglecting your work and duties in the material world.

"Trying" to meditate. This creates an inner dialog in your mind and prevents meditation from happening. One would-be meditator was trying so hard to meditate "successfully" that she realized she was saying "chest rising, chest *failing*" to herself!

One of the greatest of these dangers, detours, and delusions is that of *being misled by a guru.* With the current proliferation of people teaching others how to meditate or to become enlightened, I would urge you to beware of those teachers or gurus who—

Charge large sums of money and/or claim supernormal powers. "No true master of meditation will take one penny for his teaching. No true master makes any claim, or allows any claim to be made on his behalf, to abnormal powers or achievement," says Christmas Humphreys, the long-time head of the Buddhist Society in London.

Have poor relationships with the major people in their lives.

Believe their way is the only way and bad-mouth other gurus.

Enjoy a sense of importance from being a guru and having disciples.

Tell you that they are teaching you some secret knowledge (probably because you are already so special) that you must swear to keep secret. All of the esoteric knowledge is available in written form for those who will seek it out.

Attempt to make you dependent on them and their advice. A good teacher is one who strengthens your own ability to make decisions for yourself and who helps you to find your own guru within.

Claim to have learned it all. There is no end, no stopping point, so find a teacher who knows and acknowledges that he is still learning. (The phrase "perfect master" is semantic nonsense.) According to Ramana Maharshi, a true guru "never sees any difference between himself and others and is quite free from the idea that he is the Enlightened or the Liberated One, while those around him are in bondage or the darkness of ignorance."

I would like to postulate that Jung's *shadow* has a flip side in the collective unconscious of each of us. That is the Irridescence, or one's shining side. If you are not in touch with your own goodness, saintliness, compassion, altruism, and all those other good things, then you will project them onto the nearest candidate for sainthood. In this manner you can make very ordinary people, even con men, into saints and gurus.

Exercise for Reclaiming Your Irridescence

Visualize someone whom you admire, respect, idealize.

What are his most praiseworthy traits?

Recall some incidents when she behaved in a particularly altruistic or saintly way.

Now try these traits and behaviors on for size. To what extent do they fit you? To what extent do you possess similar qualities and virtues?

I don't believe any of us can recognize the saintly qualities in another unless we possess those qualities in some measure ourselves. As Ram Dass says, "When a pickpocket meets a saint, all he sees are his pockets."

After you have learned how to find your center and to trust being there, you will find that you can check in there whenever there is a crisis or you need to make a decision. If you need an answer to a question, you might try this fantasy exercise:

Chinese Temple Exercise

First, get in a meditative position and observe your breathing.

Next, imagine that you are climbing many stone steps up a steep hill. At the top of the hill there is a Chinese temple with a pagoda roof. There are doors in the center of each of the four sides. On each door is carved a golden dragon. Push open one of the doors and enter the temple.

There is no furniture inside, just many scrolls in racks like the stacks in your public library. Select one of the scrolls. Take it to the center of the room where there is a bright light coming down from the raised skylight. Unroll the scroll. Read it and find the answer to your question.

If you are not already a meditator, I hope that this chapter will give you the encouragement to start. Perhaps one of the methods I described instantly appealed to you. If not, I would suggest that you start with breath mindfulness. Remember that you are in charge of selecting your place and time, and you are in charge of disciplining your mind and attention to stay with the task. The rest will happen to you; you don't have to "try" for it.

An excellent description of the process is given by Eugen Herrigel in *Zen in the Art of Archery:*

> The more one concentrates on breathing, the more the external stimuli fade into the background. They sink away in a kind of muffled roar which one hears with only half an ear at first, and in the end one finds it no more disturbing than the distant roar of the sea, which, once one has grown accustomed to it, is no longer perceived . . . One only knows and feels that one breathes . . .
>
> This exquisite state of unconcerned immersion in one-self is not, unfortunately, of long duration . . . As though sprung from nowhere, moods, feelings, desires, worries and even thoughts incontinently rise up, in a meaningless jumble, and the more far-fetched and preposterous they are, and the less they have to do with that on which one has fixed one's consciousness, the more tenaciously they hang on . . . the only successful way of rendering this disturbance inoperative is to keep on breathing, quietly and unconcernedly, to enter into friendly relations with whatever appears on the scene, to accustom oneself to it, to look at it equably and at last grow weary of looking . . . [Ultimately one achieves] the feeling, otherwise experienced only in rare dreams, of extraordinary lightness, and the rapturous certainty of being able to summon up energies in any direction . . .

CHAPTER 8

AWARENESS AND THE ART OF BEING IN THE NOW

> To reject one's own experience is to arrest one's
> own development, and to deny one's own experi-
> ence is to put a lie into the lips of one's own
> life and it is no less than the denial of the soul.
> —Oscar Wilde

What is your conception of TIME? Do you see it, perhaps, as some endless ticker tape coming from some unseen place at your left and proceeding to some unseen place off to your right? If so, which portions of this ticker tape would you designate as "the past," "the present," and "the future"? And how would you delineate the boundaries?

Westerners typically seem to have some such graphic image of Time; their past as well as their future seems as real as the present. And Time seems to flow from one moment to the next with no boundaries.

Let me propose a different image: This moment . . . this microsecond . . . is all there is. The past is fiction, the future is prediction. Of course, by the time you have read that last sentence, several microseconds went by (and many, many more if you interrupted your reading to answer the telephone, get a cup of tea, or speak to someone else in the room!) Imagine that in each microsecond the world and all its reality is created anew and that if you were sufficiently attentive you could observe and even participate in that creation.

Too heavy? Let's run it through a different way. "Now" is what's here at this moment, what we can *be aware of RIGHT NOW*. What are you aware of at this moment . . . this book . . . the look of the print on this page . . . your hands holding the book . . . your posture as you're sitting in a chair or lying in bed or standing in a bookstore . . . sounds in your environment . . . possible irritation with all these dots . . . ? All of these are your awarenesses, and the more fully cognizant you are of your awarenesses, the more fully you are living in the NOW.

For people who like categories and taxonomies, awareness can be divided into three kinds:

1. *Head chatter*, or the thinking, judging, planning, remembering, anticipating, analyzing, that occupy the majority of most people's awareness time. At this moment I'm thinking, "Can I finish this chapter today? I want to give it to Jean to type tomorrow." And I realize that pressuring thoughts like this will only impede the flow, and I decide to stay with the writing and when the chapter is finished, it will be finished.

2. *Sensory awareness*, or any information coming to you from the outside by way of your eyes, ears, nose, and taste buds. Right now I'm aware of the look of these letters I have just written, of the blue of my sweater, of the gold carpet in the background. I hear the sound of children playing and of the wind blowing.

3. *Body awareness*, or any messages coming to you from your muscles, joints, stomach, intestines, genitalia, and so on. Right now, I'm aware of my slumped posture in the chair (and I'm changing it). I'm aware of my back itching and feeling warm in the sweater (but not enough to stir me to go change).

Most of this book has been devoted to an examination of your mind chatter. Let's now do some exercises to identify your sensory awareness and your body awareness.

Sensory Awareness

Most of the following exercise on sensory awareness is done with your eyes closed. If possible, have someone read it to you, pausing at the dots. Or if that's not possible, read it aloud yourself onto a tape and play the tape whenever you are ready to do the exercise. Allow 30 minutes for the exercise.

Sensory Awareness Exercise

Look around the room (or wherever you are). Observe each thing as it is . . . notice form and textures . . . and color . . . and light and shadow . . . Notice juxtaposition of forms . . . If you find you are labeling things, giving them a name ("The chair is green, that's a photograph, the lamp looks Mexican."), then you're on a taxonomy trip.

There's nothing wrong with naming things, but it does put you back into your head. For this exercise try to just SEE things . . . as an infant with no names to call things . . . Are you noticing things and making further comments to yourself? Such as "That picture's crooked" or "That ventilator is dusty." If you are, you're back into your mind chatter and making judgments instead of just SEEING . . . Try relaxing your eyes, maybe let them get a little out of focus . . . try looking at some very small object, possibly some smaller part of a larger whole, maybe one tuft in the rug, or one square centimeter of upholstery . . . stay with this one place . . . What do you really see there? Can you let yourself merge with the object you are viewing?

Now—close your eyes. What do you see now? . . . Be aware of any after-images . . . and listen . . . What do you hear? . . . There are probably sounds that you now realize were there all along, but that you weren't aware of when you were concentrating on seeing . . . Put all your attention into your listening . . . realize all the minute and subtle sounds that you can pick up when you really attend . . . Suppose that you had been brought to this place drugged and blindfolded and had just now regained consciousness. By using just your ears, realize how much you know about where you are . . . in a city or in the country? . . . in a building or out-of-doors? . . .

with other people around you or alone? . . . If there are other people present, what can you know about them by the sounds that you hear? . . .

Now, still keeping your eyes closed, put all your attention into your sense of smell. What does the air smell like? . . . Smell your hand. Does it smell familiar, or strange? If you didn't know it was your own hand, could you recognize it by its smell? . . . Now smell your hair if it's long enough to reach to your nose . . . and smell some of your clothing . . . and smell your armpits . . . Smell objects in your environment . . . What can you know about them by their smell? . . . The carpet—how recently was it vacuumed? . . . Is the purse made of leather or vinyl? . . .

Now, still keeping your eyes closed, put a small piece of food in your mouth (apple, strawberry, half a segment of orange perhaps) . . . Did you smell it before you tasted it? Chew it thoroughly, slowly . . . notice how it tastes different later than it did at the beginning . . . After you swallow it, be aware of the aftertaste . . .

Now, without moving your hands, be aware of what information you are getting from them, especially from your fingertips. If this were your only source of information, what would you know about the outside world, just from your fingertips? . . . Now move your hands so that they touch one another. Have one of your hands explore the other . . . See what this strange hand feels like, explore the contours of the bones, the lumps, the valleys, fingernails, cuticles . . . examine the texture of the skin . . . Now shift the focus of your awareness from the hand that is doing the exploring to the hand that is being explored . . . Once your focus is shifted, you may also want to change the quality of the touch so that your hand feels as if it is being caressed rather than explored . . . Experiment with the degree of pressure that the receiving hand appreciates most, and with the type and speed of movement . . . Now return your focus to the exploring hand . . . Which modality do you prefer? Switch back to the hand that is being caressed . . . Are you able to switch the focus of your awareness on demand? . . .*

. . . Now notice which hand you designated to be the exploring hand and which hand to be the one-being-caressed . . . Have your hands switch tasks so that the exploring hand becomes the one being caressed and the formerly receptive hand becomes the one that explores. Again, put your full attention on the hand that is doing the exploring . . . See what this new hand feels like, explore its bones, muscles, skin, fingernails . . . Now switch your focus to the hand that was being explored . . . see how it feels being explored, touched, caressed . . . Is this as easy to do as it was with the original pair? . . . Or do your hands feel some resistance to their new roles? . . .

Now let your hands start exploring your face as if it were the face of a stranger and you were a blind person . . . See what new things you can learn about the face that you look at in the mirror every day . . . Now shift the focus of your attention to your face and see how it feels to be felt by these fingers and hands . . . Experiment with the kind of stroking that feels best . . . what pressure of touch, what speed of movement . . . what direction of movement . . . what portion of hands and fingers . . . As before, switch back and forth between attending to what your hands feel and what your face feels . . . Now extend your area of exploration to your neck, arms, body, legs, feet . . . Again, alternate your focus between exploring and experiencing the touch . . . Compare the experience of being touched in those areas of your body

---

*This is analagous to the standard picture in the introductory psychology textbooks of the pretty young woman wearing a big hat who, when you change the focus of your attention, becomes an old hag.

that are clothed with places where your hands contact your skin directly. Which touch is more stimulating? More pleasant?

Now, with your eyes still closed, explore your environment with your hands . . . the area right around you . . . your chair . . . the carpet . . . any belongings that are within reach . . . as you feel like it, move out and explore this room or area . . . Those objects that you earlier explored with your eyes, now learn to know them with your hands . . . See how you feel voyaging out from your perch without the security of your open eyes . . . Are you crawling? . . . or do you feel secure enough to walk? . . . Notice how you are using your hands and your ears to guide you . . . If you're walking, how fast do you feel comfortable to move? . . . Continue around your room or area, exploring whatever you wish to explore . . . If you're alone, do you experience any sense of danger in doing this with your eyes closed? . . . If you're with others, how do you feel about encountering other people or the possibility of encountering them? Remember that You're in Charge—and if you're doing something you don't want to do, you have a choice . . .

Now . . . still keeping your eyes closed . . . start making your way back to the spot from which you started . . . Notice the cues you use to orient yourself . . . See if you can position yourself exactly as you were before you started your journey.

Now . . . open your eyes . . . what do you see?

If you are doing this with others, take some time now to share that experience. Take turns telling each other what you learned. If you are doing this alone, take this time to write down your experiences.

I have done this exercise with more than a hundred groups, and it is invariably a most meaningful experience for them. Different people find different parts of the exercise remarkable, depending usually upon the areas in which they had previously been unaware. Some people remark on how vivid colors seem when they open their eyes. Many people have gotten an understanding of how sensorily rich the world of the blind can be and have lost their fears of becoming blind. Some people learn that their two hands function very differently; one hand (typically the right hand in righthanded people) may elect to explore and may disdain being caressed. For others this may have been their first experience in totally tasting a food. What's important is NOT what others experience but what YOU experience.

Reading here what others have experienced or hearing others recount their experiences are of value for you only as it helps you notice what you have experienced and hadn't noticed that you noticed. (Or perhaps you thought it wasn't important enough to notice. Many awarenesses seem trivial to a mind that has been trained to be profound and scholarly!) Perhaps your Critic subpersonality is commenting that you didn't have such-and-such an awareness and therefore you must be _____. (I'm not going to reinforce your Critic by filling the blank with any negative labels.)

Again, what's important is what YOU experience . . . including your awareness of your Critic and any judgmental remarks it may make.

Body Awareness

Here's an exercise to help you get in touch with the messages your body has for you. Again, it's best to have someone read this to you, pausing at the dots. If that's not possible, read it aloud yourself onto a tape and play the tape whenever you wish to do the exercise. Allow 30 minutes.

Body Awareness Exercise

Get into a comfortable position and close your eyes. Be aware of which parts of your body are touching the chair, floor, bed, etc. Allow yourself to relax into their support. Feel them raising up to support your body . . . Now notice how you are breathing. Don't try to change it. Notice how you *are* breathing . . . Notice your air going in and your air going out . . . Notice what parts of your body move as you breathe . . . Now I will start mentioning different parts of your body. As you breathe in, I want you to focus your attention on that part that I've most recently mentioned. As you breathe out, let all your body tension go out with your breath . . . First your forehead. Are you frowning or is it smooth? . . . Your eyelids . . . closed or fluttering? . . . Your eyeballs . . . still or moving? Any after-images? . . . Your cheeks . . . relaxed or smiling? . . . Your ears . . . the same temperature as the rest of your face? hotter? cooler? . . . Your nose . . . can you feel the little hairs in your nostrils move as your breath passes by? Your lips . . . moist or dry? Closed or parted? Your tongue . . . where is it lying? What is it touching? . . . Your teeth . . . check each one out. Any feeling of pressure from food caught between teeth? How recently brushed do they feel to you? . . . Your neck. Any feeling of fatigue from having to hold your head up? Or does your head feel well-balanced on your neck? . . . Be aware of all of your vertebrae from the big ones right under your skull to the coccyx at the end of your spine . . . What line does your spine make right now? . . . Be aware of the muscles that are attached to your spine. Is your back tense or relaxed? . . . Be aware of your shoulders. Are they raised slightly, or do they hang loose? . . . Your shoulder blades in the back, are they parallel with your back or sticking out at an angle? . . . Be aware of your shoulder sockets and without moving your arms, visualize yourself rotating your

arms in their sockets . . . Be aware of your upper arms
. . . your elbows . . . bent or straight? . . . Your lower
arms . . . your wrists . . . your hands . . . your fingers
. . . Any tension there?

Now be aware of your heart beating. Don't try to count
the beats, just be aware of the rhythm . . . Now listen
for an echo of this rhythm in other places in your body—
your temples, your throat, your wrists, your groin, your
ankles.

Be aware of your breath coming into your body again.
Follow it through your nose, down your trachea, and
into your lungs. Watch them expand and then deflate . . .
Now swallow and be aware of your esophagus . . . Your
stomach. Any activity here? How long since your last
meal? Hungry yet for the next one? If so, *how* do you
know that? . . . Be aware of your small intestines. Any
activity here? . . . Your large intestines, first the part
ascending on your right side, then the part going across,
then the part going down on your left side with its funny
S-shaped curve. Any action going on here? . . . Your
rectum, any sense of fullness here? How soon will you
want to evacuate your bowel? . . . Your anus . . . is it
held together tightly or is it relaxed?

Now be aware of your kidneys, those two bean-shaped
organs in the small of your back . . . Be aware of the
ducts leading to your bladder and your bladder itself.
Any sense of fullness here? How soon do you imagine
you will want to urinate? . . . Now—men, be aware of
your testicles, and women, your ovaries. How are your
testicles lying? Are you "dressed left or right," as the
fancy tailors ask? Women, how soon will you ovulate
again and on which side? . . . Women, be aware of your
uterus . . . Men, your penis, and women, your clitoris
and labia . . . Now be aware of your pelvic bones that
cradle these internal organs. Is your pelvis tilted? . . .

Be aware of your hip sockets. Without moving your legs, imagine your legs raising and lowering . . . Imagine yourself describing circles in the air with your feet, first, circles rotating inward toward the center . . . then circles rotating outwards.

Now be aware of your thighs . . . your knees. What temperature are they? Warmer, colder, or the same temperature as the rest of your legs? . . . Your calves. Any tension in the back of your calves? . . . Your ankles. Flex your feet and see what degree of movement you possess . . . Your feet and your toes. If you're wearing shoes or stockings, see if your toes feel cramped . . .

Now take a journey back up your body from your toes to the top of your head. Compare your left side to the right side. See if it's the same or if it feels different. See if you can be aware of your body all the way up. Or are there any "holes" in your awareness?

Now take a moment to experience your body as an integrated whole. Say, this is me,* this is (and say your name). This is where I live . . .

Now take a deep breath, stretch, and get up slowly.

What was your experience? If you are like many others, you may have become aware of sensations in your body that you are not noticing before. A cold nose, perhaps, or warm knees. Possibly muscles that you were holding tight at a time when there was no work for them to do. In the trip back up the body, some people experience their left and right sides quite differently; others find that they are less aware of themselves on one side than on the other. If you find that there are parts of your body

---

*You super-alert readers may have noticed that this statement is seemingly opposite to the "I have a body, but I am not my body" statement in the Disidentification Exercise. Not really. You have to be aware of your body and own it before you can disidentify from it. Disidentifying is not denying.

that are "missing" from your awareness, you could have a dialogue with them.

The last part of the exercise where you experience your body as a whole is a most important part. One young man started weeping silently at the phrase, "This is where I live." He had not been appreciating his body and had been neglecting and abusing it. He then did some dialoguing with various parts of his body, listened to "their" complaints about his poor treatment of them, and agreed to exercise more, smoke less, and eat better. This reconciliation work was so moving that most of the group was crying a little.

Living in the NOW

Once you have learned the art of self observation, you should find that you are tuned into NOW a greater percentage of the time. You will be aware of entertaining a PAST thought (nostalgia for past events or people, resentments or grievances) and quickly realize that that is *not* what is happening NOW. Similarly, you will be able to identify a FUTURE thought, deal with it, and dismiss it.

Many people come into therapy with the complaint, "I'm not happy," and ask for a recipe to achieve happiness. After all, isn't the "pursuit of happiness" an inalienable right of all Americans, according to our Declaration of Independence? I believe that the *pursuit* of happiness is futile . . . happiness is something that you realize you are experiencing NOW . . . whether it's when gardening, nursing a baby, watching a sunset, talking with a friend, writing, or even washing the dishes. For me, it's the experience of realizing how totally, one-pointedly involved I am in some activity to the exclusion of all else. And, of course, at the moment of this realization, I have interrupted the experience and the happiness peak is already passed. Life is a river; you cannot stop it to examine its substance. For once you know the quality of one moment, it is already a past moment and you are spending your current moment in remembering and analyzing the past.

When you are truly in the NOW, you may not be able to describe your experience well afterwards, as you're not laying down the words for your "book review" of the experience. Ernest Schachtel describes two different perceptual modes of viewing the world. In the subject-centered mode, the perceiver views the object from the perspective of how it will serve his needs and is very conscious of himself as he is viewing the object. In the object-centered mode, the perceiver opens himself totally to the object with all his senses and sensibilities, leaving behind his egocentric thoughts and strivings, and permits himself to experience the object without the limitations of labels and familiarity.

The subject-centered viewer asks of the object, "How can I use you?" Or, "How can I protect myself against you?" The object-centered viewer asks, "Who or what are you, who are part of this same world of which I am a part?"

The subject-centered viewer will not truly experience a trip to Europe; he will "see" Europe through the viewfinder of his camera in terms of the slides he will show his friends upon his return home.

The object-centered viewer will stumble out of the cinema still entranced with the experience and unprepared for the critical questions of his subject-centered companion who "saw" the movie in terms of the sentences of the movie review he was preparing to give his friends the next day.

Some museum-goers will first look quickly to see the name of the painter before looking at the painting; thus they can orient themselves to what they are about to perceive or—possibly—decide whether the painting is worth bothering to look at!

The object-centered viewer, on the other hand, allows herself to become absorbed in the painting, to feel almost at one with it. She might then realize that this is a painting she has seen and enjoyed before and can possibly even identify, but her current perception is not dulled by past "knowledge" of the picture.

Here's an exercise to help you develop your object-centered perception:

Object-Centered Perception

Select an object that is very familiar to you, that you see every day . . . your front door . . . your spouse . . . a fork . . . your cat . . . your own face in the mirror . . .

Look at this object (or person) as if you've never seen it before, and have no words with which to describe it. Examine it . . . with your eyes, ears, nose, fingers . . . Notice how many new things you discover about it . . . If you find yourself making judgments (especially in the case of your spouse!), see if these judgments are springing from your "needs" of this person or object.

Are you experiencing any expectations that the object remain familiar, or any resistance to seeing it differently? Do you discover any surprises about this supposedly well-known object?

CHAPTER 9

YOU'RE IN CHARGE OF YOUR PHYSICAL HEALTH

Why, you may ask, have I included a chapter on your physical health in a book that deals with learning the art of self-observation? Mind and body are one unit, and the health of your body will affect your mind and your ability to be in charge. This being a self-therapy book, I will never see you, the reader; and I would feel remiss if I did not alert you to some of those principal areas—breathing, food, exercise, sleep—that can influence your mental and emotional life.

The health that we have *now* is largely* the result of our actions of the past—how we have chosen to breathe and to move, what we have chosen to put into our bodies, and what thoughts and attitudes we have chosen to have. Today, now, we are determining our future health. You're in charge!

A. Breath: The Number One Intake

Breathing is the most important thing you do every day. It's also very likely something that you don't pay much attention to and possibly don't do well. According to ancient Chinese medicine, every illness can be attributed to inadequate circula-

---

* There are, of course, genetic faults and environmental hazards that are beyond our control.

tion or lack of breath. Stop right now and notice *how* you are breathing:

Breath Awareness Exercise

What parts of your body are moving?
In what order are they moving?
How many breaths per minute?
Are you breathing through your nose, your mouth, or both?
Are you exhaling *all* of your air?

Now lie down on your back.

Have your knees up with the soles of your feet on the floor or the mattress.

Inhale gently and comfortably through your nostrils, letting your abdomen rise at the beginning of the inhalation, then letting your chest rise, and finally, as the air fills the horns of the lungs under your collarbones, feeling your shoulders lifting a little.

When it comes time to exhale, let the breath out slowly with a s-s-s sound. (Remember stretching the neck of a balloon and letting the air hiss its way out for as long as possible?) Suck in your abdomen and let your diaphragm squeeze some more air out. You may find that your head is bowing forward onto your chest.

When you absolutely cannot hiss any more, let go, . . . and notice how your abdomen and chest bound up with Nature's air rushing in to replenish you.

This exercise is a good one for demonstrating that the major work in breathing is the job of *exhaling*. Many people mistakenly believe that the effort of breathing comes with inhaling (and these people are apt to be afraid that they won't get enough breath). It's important to breathe out as much as possible of the old, foul air, rather than storing it in your lungs. You will then have room for the maximum quantity of fresh air with your next incoming breath. Your body's survival system is designed to make you breathe in *automatically* as soon as there is room from exhaling. As you exhale, you create an empty space; Nature then sends fresh air flowing in to fill the vacuum.

The best method of breathing is called Complete Breathing, which directs air into all parts of your lungs:

Complete Breathing

Stand or sit with your spine erect.

Breathe through your nostrils, first filling the lower part of your lungs by pushing out on your belly wall. (If you suck in your stomach as you breathe in, then you can fill only the upper part of your lungs, which is less than half of your potential air space.)

Next, let the middle part of your lungs fill by pushing out your lower ribs and your breastbone (or sternum).

Next, fill the highest portion of your lungs by letting your shoulders lift a little and your abdomen draw in a little.

Let your breath stay still a few seconds.

Then exhale slowly by drawing your abdomen in still further and letting it lift upward slowly.

You will need to inhale a series of Complete Breaths several times a day in order to develop this style of breathing. You may have to practice in front of a mirror with your hand on your stomach to feel the movement in order to de-program yourself from the typical pattern of the urban westerner, whose stomach goes *in* with the inhalation. Complete Breathing is not a weird or freaky breathing practice. It is the style of the healthy savage; it's also the style of the healthy infant in our culture. Once you have learned Complete Breathing, I predict that you will find the old method uncomfortable; it will feel constrained and like "starvation time."

Check yourself as you read: Do you keep your mouth firmly closed when you inhale, or are you a mouth-breather? How do you breathe when you're asleep? Waking with a dry throat and wanting a glass of water is a clue that you may be breathing through your mouth.

I hope you have already begun to notice how your breathing pattern changes according to your emotional state. When you are afraid, you are likely to breathe very shallowly or to hold your breath. This will not help you in your fear state, because you need constant rhythmic input of breath to give you support. So one of the best ways to help yourself when you realize you are feeling anxious is to ask yourself, "How am I breathing?" And then gently but firmly initiate a pattern of deep, rhythmic breathing. Concentrating on your breathing will calm your mind, and the improved physiology of your breathing will change your body chemistry in ways that will give you relief.

Rhythmic Breathing

Sit with your back erect and your hands resting comfortably in your lap.

Have one hand feel the pulse in your other wrist and start counting: 1, 2, 3, 4, 5, 6; 1, 2, 3, 4, 5, 6, and so on until you get in tune with the rhythm of your heartbeat.

Then start Complete Breathing.

Slowly inhale a Complete Breath to the count of six pulse units.

Hold the breath for three pulse units.

Exhale slowly for six pulse units.

Rest between breaths for three pulse units.

Inhale a Complete Breath for six pulse units. And so on for several cycles. Don't fatigue yourself doing this.

Do this deep, rhythmic breathing *slowly*. If you breathe quickly, gulping the air (frequently through your mouth), as if in fear that you won't get enough air, you may hyperventilate and get *too* much oxygen into your system. This will make you feel panicky and you may gulp even more air. The cure for this vicious circle is to put your head (or at least your nose and your mouth) into a brown paper bag. Breathe in your own exhaled air until the proper balance of carbon dioxide and oxygen has been reached. (You'll know this by the easing of your feeling of panic. It will take only a few minutes.) People who are apt to hyperventilate are those same people who don't exhale fully. They also may be people who have a feeling of deprivation and want to grab all they can before the supply runs out.

Rhythmic Breathing is an excellent exercise to do whenever you are feeling anxious, or not centered, or just generally and mysteriously "out of sorts."

B. Food: The Number Two Intake

> A full belly is the mother of all evil.
> —Benjamin Franklin

> Man lives on one-quarter of what he eats.
> On the other three-quarters lives his doctor.
> —Inscription in an Egyptian pyramid,
> ca. 3000 BC

So many people in the United States are so preoccupied with food—what to eat, how much to eat, how to prepare it, which foods to avoid, etc.—that I hesitate to add any more printed words on the subject. Another sector of the population denies any interest in the subject; these people stoke their bodies with whatever commodity is available at the nearest fast-food stand and resist any warnings that certain foods could be detrimental to their health. Even the first category may have difficulty with the following exercise:

24-Hour Food and Drink Accounting

Think back over the past 24 hours, starting with now and working backwards.

Write down everything you have eaten. This includes snacks, "tastes" of someone else's dish. (Just because he ordered the crepes suzette doesn't mean he gets to keep all the calories and other sugar-consequences if you share the dessert!)

Estimate amounts.

If you have jars of nuts, seeds, raisins, etc., within easy reach on a kitchen shelf, be sure to include how many times you opened a jar and how much you took out each time.

Let's get more technical. How much sugar would you say you ingested in the last 24 hours? How much salt?

What were the ingredients in the salad dressing? What spices were used in the preparation of the various dishes?

Here's the hardest part: What have you had to drink? How many cups of coffee? How many glasses of water? of orange juice? of wine? How many beers? How many cocktails? Highballs?

I'm willing to bet that you can't answer all of the questions with complete certainty. And to the extent that you can't, you're failing to be in charge of your health.

Let's look at the specific effects of several different foods.

Sugar. This is probably the worst offender. A refined substance, it is absorbed too rapidly and too traumatically by the body, causing the endocrine balance to become upset. This leads to hypoglycemia (a condition of an estimated 49 per cent of the

American population), which is characterized by any or all of the following symptoms when the blood-sugar level is low: dizziness, fainting, blackouts, headaches, fatigue, irritability, inability to concentrate, loss of appetite, loss of sexual interest, allergies, blurred vision, impotency, depression, cold hands and feet, nervous exhaustion, tremors and drowsiness. Drs. Cheraskin and Ringdorf suggest—and not facetiously—that candy bar manufacturers be forced to print this warning on their wrappers: "This product can be dangerous to your mental health." If these symptoms sound familiar, I would earnestly suggest that you take charge and put yourself on a hypoglycemic diet, regardless of the results of your glucose-tolerance test. I've had many people in my practice with a "normal" score on that test who were able to alter their mental and emotional states by a change in diet.

Coffee. I don't have anything good to say about coffee, either. To begin with, the caffeine gives a jolt to the sympathetic nervous system and sends undue amounts of insulin and adrenalin into the blood stream, thus hastening the onset of hypoglycemia and all the low blood sugar level symptoms listed above. Secondly, it's addictive. Once you are hooked, you will need more and more coffee to give you that nice "lift."

A Michigan psychiatrist has introduced the term "caffeinism" to describe the symptoms of anxiety and depression among hospitalized psychiatric patients who were high caffeine consumers. ("High" was classified as more than 750 milligrams of caffeine a day; an average cup of American coffee contains 100 mg., a cup of tea has 50 to 75 mg.) What's your daily caffeine consumption?

If you decide to kick the coffee habit, be prepared to suffer certain withdrawal symptoms—headaches, sleepiness, nervousness, depression (although these symptoms can be ameliorated by taking large quantities of vitamin C). It's probably best to cut down one cup a day until you reach the one-cup level. Stay with one cup of coffee for three or four days (that first one in the morning, maybe?) and then kick it, too. Chocolate, the cola beverages, and certain medications* also contain caffeine.

White Flour, White Rice, and other Refined Starches such as Macaroni, Spaghetti, and Pizza Dough. Grains are good for

---

* Anacin, Coricidin, Darvon Compound, Empirin Compound, Excedrin, Four-Way Cold Tablets, to name a few.

you—whole grains, that is. Wheat and other grains have been a staple ingredient of the human diet ever since we settled down and became agricultural beings. Then came the industrial revolution and the invention of fancy and efficient mills that could remove all of those troublesome parts of the grain that had prevented its being a long-storage commodity.

When the brown wheat berry is trampled, rolled, tortured and bleached into "clean" white flour, more than twenty different vitamins, minerals and amino acids are lost. Especially important among them are: thiamine (B1), niacin (B3), pyridoxine (B6), B12, pantothenic acid, biotin, folic acid, vitamin E, magnesium, and potassium. Low concentrations of any of these in your brain can lead to symptoms of "mental illness" or emotional unrest. For instance, niacin deficiencies can cause such extreme disturbances as hallucination, catatonia, and acute delirium. Magnesium-deficient people are apt to be "high strung," jumpy at the slightest noise, and unable to sleep. Those lacking pantothenic acid are particularly vulnerable to stress, easily upset, and irritable. Large quantities of refined sugars and starches (also large amounts of alcohol) can bring on a thiamine deficiency, which is characterized by nervousness, fatigue, depression, mood changes, memory lapses, and difficulty in concentration. (If these symptoms fit you, don't rush off and start taking large quantities of vitamin B1, as that can induce a deficiency of some of the other important B fractions. You'll need to take the whole B complex.) A lack of vitamin B6 causes irritability, quarrelsomeness, trembling, and tension. And so on.

Alcohol. Since alcohol is a fermented sugar (naturally occurring in barley, rye, grapes, etc.) everything said about sugar applies here, too. Excessive drinking leads to severe vitamin deficiencies, especially B1 and B6. High alcohol consumption leads to irreversible brain damage. (When nerve cells in the brain die, they do not regenerate.)

The whole topic of alcoholism is a vast one and beyond the scope of this book. There is more than one kind of alcoholism, and, therefore, more than one type of appropriate treatment. Some alcoholics are literally driven to drink by their hypoglycemia. When they go on a strict hypoglycemia diet and their blood sugar levels become normal, they stop wanting to drink. Another group seems to profit from the megavitamin formula of massive doses of niacin, vitamin C, and glutamine. And a third group does well on the juice cleansing fast and the lacto-vegetarian diet prescribed by Dr. Paavo Airola. Many profit by joining the program of Alcoholics Anonymous.

"Going on a Diet"

So what can you do? Go on a diet? If so, which diet? We've had the drinking man's diet, the rice diet, the bran diet, the all protein diet, the raw foods diet, Dr. Adkins' diet, the grapefruit diet.* Any diet that does not contain adequate quantities of the necessary vitamins, minerals, and trace elements can be injurious to your physical and mental health. Obviously then, all of these one-food or one-category diets are dangerous. Dr. Emanuel Cheraskin suggests that indiscriminate dieting is the cause of many of the current mental and emotional complaints: nervousness, depression, dizziness, anxiety, poor memory, paranoia, hostility. In experiments in Minnesota, all of these symptoms were produced in healthy subjects who adhered to a restricted diet for an extended period of time.

I'd like to suggest that "going on a diet" is a poor phrase. It implies a future event, something that you will have to structure and possibly make an effort to do. The thought of this may be quite discouraging and tiring. Your diet is what you eat, *are eating, do eat.* You are already "on" the diet that you are on right now! Every minute you are making a choice to eat something or not to eat something. (How many times while you were reading the section about foods did you consider having something to eat right then? How many times did you actually eat?) If you don't like the diet that you are on, there is a new minute and a new choice-point coming up, and you can change your diet. *You're in charge!*

If you went on a doughnut binge two hours ago, this doesn't mean that all is lost and you might as well have two colas and three brownies now. Two hours ago is two hours ago, and now is now. If you want to be on a sugar-free diet now, you make the choice to say "no" to the cola and brownies now. Tell your Critic that the doughnuts are history. Large quantities of vitamin

---

*The *Los Angeles* magazine did a satirical article on the different lifestyles in various suburbs. They chose "diet" as one of the several categories (along with makes of automobile, recreation, alcoholic beverage, favorite book, etc.) used to stereotype the communities.

C can help people who are trying to break addictions to certain foods.

History can be useful as an aid to you in making your on-going choices about diet. I'd like to suggest that you conscientiously keep a record of everything that you put into your mouth for a week. At the end of that time review the record. With the data right in front of you, I think you'll get a clearer answer to the second magic question, "What do I want to eat right now"? If you are addicted to either caffeine or nicotine, my hunch is that you will not remember accurately, and that keeping an ongoing record will give you some surprising facts.

DAY _____

Include ingredients of all sauces, salad dressings, casseroles, etc., kind of cooking oil, bread and spread; and record approximate quantities.

Breakfast   Lunch   Dinner

Snacks

Cups of Coffee	1	2	3	4	5	6	7	8	9	10
Cups of Tea	1	2	3	4	5	6	7	8	9	10
Glasses Water (including herb tea)	1	2	3	4	5	6	7	8	9	10
Cigarettes Smoked	1	2	3	4	5	6	7	8	9	10
(the ones you bum as well as the ones you buy!)	11	12	13	14	15	16	17	18	19	20
Sticks of Gum Chewed	1	2	3	4	5	6	7	8	9	10
Glasses of Wine	1	2	3	4	5	6				
Cans of Beer (size?)	1	2	3	4	5	6				
Cocktails	1	2	3	4	5	6				
Tall Drinks	1	2	3	4	5	6				
Salt Intake (est. tsps.)	1	2	3	4	5	6				
Sugar Intake (est. tsps.)	1	2	3	4	5	6				

If you ate any foods containing the following, circle the appropriate item:

artificial colors (even if U.S. cert.)	BHA or BHT	hydrogenated fats	saccharin
artificial flavorings	calcium disodium EDTA calcium proprionate	hydrolized vegetable protein	sodium carboxy-methylcellulose
benzoic acid		MSG	
sodium nitrite or sodium nitrate		sulfur dioxide or other sulfites	

It's Not Just What You Eat, It's Also How You Eat It

How do you eat? What is the experience of eating for you? Here's an exercise to find out (but do it at a time when you will be alone and without distractions of newspaper, radio, or conversation):

Eating with Mindfulness

Prepare a small quantity of several different foods.

In *slow motion* be aware of the kinesthetic experience of moving fork or chopsticks to a piece of food, the sensation of added weight on your utensil, and the gradual discovery by your nose of the slowly approaching food. What are the sensations in your mouth as you anticipate the arrival of the food? (This saliva contains digestive enzymes that are important for the digestion of your food. People who eat without awareness very likely are not developing adequate quantities of saliva.)

What is the first taste sensation?

How does it feel to chew this food? Which teeth do you use first? Do you pass the food around to other teeth? How do you move the food around in your mouth?

What does the food taste like after it has been mixed with saliva?

How are you breathing as you eat this bite? Through your nose? Or did you gulp some air with your mouth along with the food? (If you notice that you are doing the latter, try placing your food in your mouth during the gap after exhaling, close your mouth firmly, and breathe in as you start your chewing.)

How many times have you chewed this particular bite? Have you started swallowing any of the bite yet? Was your swallow liquid or were there solid pieces in it?

After you have swallowed all of your first bite, pause and notice the aftertaste before you go on to your second bite.

Most people are completely unaware of their eating. They are apt to have a second bite ready to shovel into the mouth before they have really tasted the first one, much less thoroughly chewed it. One of the best ways to learn to eat less (and to enjoy it more!) is to practice eating with mindfulness for at least one meal a day until you can be mindful of how you are eating despite the circumstances.

Your Overeating Subpersonality

Is overeating a problem for you? If so, here's an exercise to work on your overeating subpersonality:

Dialogue with Your Overeating Subpersonality

Look at that part of you that eats too much.
Tell her how you feel about her food binges.
Now change places and *be* her.

Justify and explain your overeating. Tell that critical part of you "why" you need to eat and what eating does for you, the very special ways in which you feel nourished by food (even two packages of Twinkies at midnight!).

Furthermore, tell that Critic what she has to supply for you that's not currently forthcoming if you stop your food binges.

Change places. See if you now understand about this overeating subpersonality of yours. (Does she have a name?) Do you see some ways in which she could nourish herself more . . . in ways other than food? . . . Develop these ideas with her.

Change places as often as needed to finish the dialog and the reconciliation.

Finally, do the disidentification exercise for this subpersonality: I have a Piggie subpersonality, but I am not she. She tends to overreact to criticism and reach for a candy bar, and so on. Make up a monologue to fit the case of *your* overeating subpersonality.

C. Smoking

Nicotine is a vasoconstrictor: that is, it causes your blood vessels to become narrower. This means less blood gets to your brain and your mental functioning becomes impaired.

Additionally, nicotine stimulates increased output of adrenalin, thus aggravating the blood-sugar cycle in hypoglycemia. And it not only interferes with vitamin C utilization but it also actually destroys some of the vitamin C in the blood. Smokers need to double their vitamin C intake just to stay even.

Also there is some evidence that the sexual performance of cigarette smokers declines more rapidly with age than that of nonsmokers.

Any smokers still reading? What are you feeling? Scared? Angry? Stubborn? Complacent?

Nonsmokers, what are you feeling? Smug and self-righteous? (If so, check quickly to see if you have addictions of your own, such as coffee, sugar, barbiturates, Darvon, Valium. Nicotine is the most difficult of all addictions to break; it's easier to give up alcohol or heroin. It's been estimated that 85–90 percent of those people living today who ever used heroin are now "clean," whereas less than one-third of those who ever smoked cigarettes have been able to stop smoking. The other two-thirds are still daily smokers.)

An Exercise in Smoking with Awareness

Make a decision that you will smoke a cigarette.

Be aware of who it is that makes that choice. *In slow motion,* reach for your cigarettes, notice the kinesthetic feel of extracting a single cigarette from the pack.

Notice every detail of your ritual of tapping the cigarette and placing it in your mouth.

How does the cigarette feel to your hand?

What is the first sensation of your lips when the cigarette is placed there?

What do you smell? Taste?

Now reach for your lighter or matches.

What sensation in your hands?

Now ignite the match or lighter. What sensations here? How do you feel about the fire you have created? Really look at it. What do you smell?

Still in slow motion, bring the flame toward your cigarette and be aware of your sensations.

Now light your cigarette, remaining acutely aware.

How does that first draw taste and smell? What are you feeling? Do you hold the smoke in your mouth awhile? Or hastily exhale it? Or deeply inhale it? Stay with the cycle of this draw of cigarette smoke until you can no longer detect it anywhere in the atmosphere.

Meanwhile, how does the cigarette feel to the hand that is holding it? Notice the smoke curling up from the end. Notice its smell.

Be aware of how you signal yourself that you want a second draw from the cigarette. Draw in the smoke with full awareness and again notice the full cycle.

Now have a dialog with your cigarette. Tell it how you are feeling about it, what you want from it.

Now be the cigarette and answer. How do you feel about how this person is smoking you? What do you want from him or her?

D. Exercise

Hardin Jones, an eminent authority in the field of aging, says that exercise is the single best thing you can do to keep young. It's also a necessary element in the life program of anyone who wishes good emotional and mental health. It's heartening to see that after several decades of devotion to the automobile, the tube, and other sedentary activities, we are rediscovering the value of exercise.

Movement Appraisal

How long have you been sitting and reading without moving?

Think back over the last two days. How much exercise have you had?

How many minutes walking? running? swimming? bicycling? strenuous dancing?

How many sustained minutes of exercise in tennis, handball, or other sports?

See what your reaction is to this last exercise. Feeling impatient? Saying, What's the point of this in a book on self-observation? Or feeling pleased with your self-appraisal?

If you are opposed to the current fad for daily running or jogging or bikeriding or swimming, and if the word *Aerobics* is anathema to you, see if you can discover your subpersonality who doesn't want to exercise. What needs is this subpersonality meeting by keeping you off the track? Perhaps it's the comfort of staying with the familiar and not exerting yourself in new ways. Perhaps it's an old fear of failure. Or what-will-people-think. (One runner-friend of mine wears a T-shirt that says, Novice Runner, Please Don't Laugh.)

Or it might be Sweet Smelling, a subpersonality that has been brainwashed by deodorant commercials and fears sweating and getting smelly. Strenuous exercise produces sweating, which helps your body eliminate poisonous wastes. For those of you who avoid sports and exercise because you don't like to sweat, here's an interesting story: There was a gathering of all the oldest people in a district in the East where age is still revered. All were over 75 and there were a number of spry folks in their 80s and 90s. Each had a different reason to offer to explain his longevity: special diets, herbs, abstinence from alcohol, use of alcohol, and so on. Finally they discovered one common denominator in their life programs: each person did something that caused him to sweat every day.

E. On Sleeping

For many people, sleep is not a problem. It's just something they do, and don't talk about. For some others, sleep, or rather "not getting enough" sleep, is a problem. In my experience, insomniacs sleep far longer and far more deeply than they are willing to admit.* In many cases they have incorporated into their psyches a message that they *should* get a certain number of hours' sleep and that if they *don't* get this much sleep, then various dire consequences will occur the next day . . . they will be tired, unable to think straight, etc. This message may have originated with a fearful parent . . . or with parents who wanted

---

*Nearly half of the people who come to the Stanford University Sleep Disorders Clinic complaining that they cannot sleep actually sleep a full 7 to 8 hours when their sleep is monitored in the laboratory.

to program the child to *their* sleep schedule, to avoid having their sleep disturbed.

Some suggestions (if you believe yourself to be an insomniac):

1. Experiment with staying up later, getting up earlier, reducing your number of in-bed hours to just those when you are sufficiently tired to fall asleep easily. See how many hours of sleep *your* body really needs and forget what the national average is, or how many hours your spouse sleeps, or what your parents said you needed. (How many years ago was that, anyway!)

2. If you wake up before you "should" wake up, don't lie there and fret and toss because you're not sleeping. Get up and do something useful. Drink some herb tea, perhaps. Don't count the hours of sleep you've had and compare that with the magic number that you "should" have. That's still another self-torture trip.

3. If you feel you really *must* go to sleep and are having difficulty, do this exercise:

Exercise for Insomnia

Put all your attention on your breathing. Notice your air going in and your air going out. Notice what parts of your body are moving as you breathe. Now on your next inhalation, focus all your awareness on your forehead. Is it tense? Relaxed? With your next inhalation, focus on your eyelids. Are they still? Fluttering? On the next inhalation, focus on your eyeballs. And so on . . . for your cheeks, nose (notice the temperature of the air going into your nostrils, and can you feel the little hairs in your nose moving from the pressure of the hair?), lips (open? parted? moist? dry?), tongue, teeth, ears (same temperature as the rest of your face? hotter? colder?), neck muscles, throat, and so on . . . through all parts of arms, hands, trunk, legs, feet. However, if you're at all tired, you probably won't make it to your waist!

---

4. Ask yourself: What is the payoff for me in being "an insomniac"? If you have trouble answering this, assume the personality of each of the members of your family in turn and let each one tell you how he feels about your being "an insomniac." Possibly you use it as a power trip to keep the house quiet, to curtail other people's activities, to get attention and sympathy. And if you're feeling angry at me right now for having written so insensitively about the plight of the insomniac, I'd suggest that you examine this matter of the payoff quite conscientiously. What subpersonality is enjoying being an insomniac?

5. Rejoice! You belong to that fortunate minority of people such as Einstein, Steinmetz, and Edison, who don't need 7 to 8 hours of sleep. Think of all that you can accomplish with your extra hours!

6. I hope you won't resort to taking pills in order to go to sleep. They won't solve your "problem" and may create another, that of dependence on the pills. A large proportion of the patients at the Stanford University Sleep Disorders Clinic suffer from insomnia caused by taking sleeping medication in increasingly larger doses.

7. If you believe that you suffer from genuine insomnia, you can seek help at a clinic that specializes in sleep disorders such as the one at Stanford University.

At the opposite end of the spectrum from the "insomniacs" are those people who sleep only too easily and use sleep as a refuge from living. If you are one of these, my best suggestion would be to ask yourself the two magic questions: What is happening right now? What do I want for myself? Then when you have identified what it is that you are running from, see what your choices are and what you want to do. Possibly you may choose to roll over and go back to sleep again! It's your choice. You're in charge!

Some people have problems from time to time in waking up and getting going. Staying in bed asleep seems so much more desirable upon first waking up! Yet once they are up and moving, the day seems fine and they then wonder about their earlier reluctance to relinquish sleep.

Sometimes this stems from not having had enough sleep . . . when the person has not allowed himself the number of hours' sleep that his body requires. Another cause can be the temporary dominance of a pessimistic subpersonality. Here again ask the two magic questions:

1. What's happening right now? What am I feeling, thinking, doing?
2. What do I want for myself right now?

If you should be in a period of persistent morning-awakening malaise, by all means record and examine your dreams and find their message for you.

F. Mind Influences

> There is no illness of the body apart from the mind.
>
> —Socrates

Your body is not an isolated system. What you think and how you react emotionally can very definitely affect your physical health. Strong emotions such as fear, rage, anger, grief—especially when denied or repressed—are an important part of the cause of a large number of "psychosomatic" illnesses.

Here's an example of how a psychosomatic disease process begins:

Whenever you perceive a threat, real or imagined, a message is flashed to a part of the brainstem called the "diencephalon." Then, in an automatic process (which began way back in the Stone Age of our evolutionary history), the diencephalon institutes its standard emergency procedures: It raises the pulse rate, the blood pressure, and the blood sugar. Your muscles may tense, you may get goosebumps, you might have to dash for the bathroom, but you won't feel hungry. This is the mobilization of the mechanisms for fight-or-flight to which we owe our survival as a species.

However, when you neither fight nor flee, your body stays perpetually mobilized for a crisis and can suffer some unfortunate consequences as a result. High blood pressure, kidney damage, heart failure, and stomach ulcers are some of the possible penalties for long-term sustained stress, according to the theory of psychosomatic disease developed by Dr. Hans Selye, an endocrinologist at the University of Montreal.

A magnification of these symptoms can occur, according to the theory of Dr. A.T.W. Simeons, when man uses his thinking brain (or cortex) to misread the perfectly normal fight-or-flight reactions of the body. "He speaks of impotence or frigidity when the sex-instinct is suppressed by fear, of indigestion when apprehensiveness kills his appetite, and of insomnia when fright keeps him awake at night . . . The increased heartbeat becomes palpitation, the rise in blood pressure he notices as a headache, the sudden elimination of waste matter he calls diarrhea or a urinary disorder." The so-clever cortex can take any noticed and labeled symptom and start worrying about it. This fear is flashed to the diencephalon, which registers "emergency" and promptly produces the symptom in question. Simeons gives an example of a healthy person who gets an acute attack of indigestion after a rage or fear-producing incident. The person, unaware of the emotion, blames the indigestion on some cherries that he ate. The next time he has some cherries his cortex is fearful and warns, "Don't eat any more, you'll be sorry!" This fear is flashed to the diencephalon, which puts an "emergency hold" onto the secretion of gastric juices and closes the pyloric valve, thus producing a stomach ache. So the person resolves, "No more cherries." At a later date another emotional upset triggers a new stomach ache. The cherry season is over, so the cortex searches out a new food villain. And so on, until the poor stomach is allowed only a limited selection of foods and has become a dyspeptic wreck.

The obvious solution here is to stay aware. Then you will know when you are frightened or angry or sad and be able to deal with these emotions rather than repressing and mislabeling them.

There are technological tools that can help here. Biofeedback instruments that measure muscular tension, skin temperature change, brainwave activity, heart rate, and blood pressure can be used to demonstrate the physiological effects of fear, anger, and other emotions. They can show which system of the person's body is most vulnerable to stress and, most important, they can be used to train the person by "interacting with the interior self" to regulate and control a long list of these physiological effects. A biofeedback student can learn to relax the muscles that cause tension headaches, to lower his blood pressure, to warm his extremities, to calm his heartbeat, and to produce the alpha brain wave of meditation at will.

Selye in his latest book has defined stress as the "non-specific response of the body to any demand made upon it," and the stressful situation can be pleasant or unpleasant. What counts is the intensity of the demand for adaptation.

Identifying Stressful Life Events

Two researchers, Drs. Holmes and Rahe, have studied the connection between stressful life events and the onset of disease (including infectious diseases and injuries) in more than 5,000 patients. They concluded that mental and physical illness are consistently preceded by a pattern of significant life changes, and they devised the following rating scale from their results:

SOCIAL READJUSTMENT RATING SCALE

	Life Event	Point Value
1.	Death of spouse	100
2.	Divorce	73
3.	Marital separation	65
4.	Jail term	63
5.	Death of close family member	63
6.	Personal injury or illness	53
7.	Marriage	50
8.	Fired at work	47
9.	Marital reconciliation	45
10.	Retirement	45
11.	Change in health of family member	44
12.	Pregnancy	40
13.	Sex difficulties	39
14.	Gain of new family member	39
15.	Business readjustment	39
16.	Change in financial state	38
17.	Death of close friend	37
18.	Change to different line of work	36
19.	Change in number of arguments with spouse	35

	Life Event	Point Value
20.	Mortgage or loan over $10,000	31
21.	Foreclosure of mortgage or loan	30
22.	Change in work responsibilities	29
23.	Son or daughter leaving home	29
24.	Trouble with in-laws	29
25.	Outstanding personal achievement	28
26.	Spouse begins or stops work	26
27.	Starting or finishing school	26
28.	Change in living conditions	25
29.	Revision of personal habits	24
30.	Trouble with boss	23
31.	Change in work hours or conditions	20
32.	Change in residence	20
33.	Change in schools	20
34.	Change in recreational habits	19
35.	Change in church activities	19
36.	Change in social activities	18
37.	Mortgage or loan under $10,000	17
38.	Change in sleeping habits	16
39.	Change in number of family get-togethers	15
40.	Change in eating habits	15
41.	Vacation	13
42.	Christmas	12
43.	Minor violation of the law	11

To find your score, think back over the past year of your life and check any of the above events that have happened to you. Add up the assigned point values. According to the research findings, a score of 150 or more will give you a 50–50 chance of developing an illness. A score of 300 or more puts you in the 90% probability bracket. I hope you noted that such supposedly pleasant life events as "outstanding personal achievement," vacations, Christmas, and marital reconciliations are considered to be stresses.

What is your score? Are there any ongoing life event stresses that you could eliminate? Do you want to eliminate them?

Possibly you thought of some other stressful life events that were not included in the scale, such as a weather disaster (unusually cold winter, hurricane, earthquake, flood, drought), robbery, jury duty, or living through a house remodeling. What value would you assign to any of these events?

Is your cortex scaring you about the possibility of illness based on your score? Watch it, remember what that robot diencephalon can do! Take a long, deep breath instead. Or do a few cycles of Rhythmic Breathing. Identify which subpersonality was temporarily dominating your cortex; and from your center, dialog with him about your health.

"Energy Follows Thought"

There is increasing clinical evidence to demonstrate the age-old esoteric belief that "energy follows thought," that your thinking can cause certain physiological changes to take place.

Visualization for Complete Health

Sit in a meditative position.

Meditate for a few minutes (any technique that you choose) until you feel very relaxed.

Now go back through your memory bank to remember peak experiences, moments at which you felt supremely happy.

Select one of these memories and relive the experience.

Send the feeling of wellbeing throughout your body, especially to any areas that have been giving you problems.

Visualize any diseases or bodily problems disappearing from the tremendous energy generated by this experience of wellbeing.

Enjoy the feeling of your body being totally well and in complete health. Imagine yourself in the future, being active, doing things with your completely healthy body.

Dr. Carl Simonton and his wife, Stephanie Mathews-Simonton, have pioneered in the use of visualization techniques with advanced cancer patients in which the person visualizes the cancer being attacked and destroyed (frequently utilizing radiation or chemotherapy as the attacking agent). Their patients who achieve reversal of the disease process are typically the ones with positive visualizations and positive attitudes. (A man who was doing poorly revealed that he visualized his cancer as a big black rat who occasionally ate one of the little yellow pills—the anticancer medication. The rat would then get sick for awhile, but always recover and then bite the patient all the harder.)

Norman Cousins, the former editor of the *Saturday Review*, came down with a very debilitating disease, ankylosing spondylitis, after his return from a very stressful trip to the Soviet Union in 1964. One specialist gave him 1 chance in 500 of recovering. Cousins remembered that Selye had written about the negative effects that are produced in the body by negative emotions; he speculated that he might achieve positive chemical changes with positive emotions. So he decided to experiment with this as a treatment and, with the cooperation of his physician, checked out of the hospital (a negative emotion place if there ever was one) and into a hotel. He substituted massive doses of vitamin C for the aspirin he had been taking, and instituted a program of laughter by watching *Candid Camera* movies and being read to out of humor anthologies. He not only lived, but made a complete recovery and plays tennis and golf and goes horseback riding. He credits his recovery to his will to live: "Since I didn't accept the verdict, I wasn't trapped in the cycle of fear, depression, and panic that frequently accompanies a supposedly incurable illness."

There has been some interesting research on the correlations between different types of personality and different diseases. Drs. Meyer Friedman and Ray Rosenman have described the kind of person whom they feel is most likely to have a heart attack. This Type A person is excessively competitive and impatient, and has a sense of urgency about deadlines (which are often unrealistic). He is typically an outgoing person, but his gregariousness often conceals a deep-seated insecurity about his own worth. To reassure himself, he keeps a numerical account of his accomplishments, (how much more money he earned last year than the year before, his standing in his graduation class, how many sales he made, e.g., or cases won, or operations performed, or sinners saved, depending on whether he is a salesman, lawyer, surgeon, or preacher), and so on. Can you think of other examples? Do you have a set of numerical gauges for measuring your progress?

Another characteristic of the Type A personality is an underlying hostility that is easily aroused under stress and most commonly directed toward employees, subordinates, family, and close friends, rarely toward the boss or other people in authority.

The most characteristic component of the Type A personality is her "hurry sickness," her feeling that she must always be doing something constructive and not "waste time." Let's see where you are with regard to time:

Dialog with Time

Have a dialog with Time, either out loud, or in writing.

Tell Time how you feel about him, what you like, what you resent, what you want from him.

Be Time and reply.

Go back and forth until you feel you have explored fully your relationship with Time.

Did you describe Time as your enemy?

Did you see him as a commodity that you wanted to make the greatest possible use of?

Did you complain of having too much time, that time was something "on your hands"?

Did you fairly quickly come to thoughts of your eventual death? One woman wrote, "You mark the length of my transit through this life. I want to have enough of you to do all the things I want to do. Most of all, I want to enjoy you." (More of this in the next chapter.)

Here are some questions that may help you pinpoint some of the games you play with Time:

1. When you are doing a routine, boring task, do you ever time yourself and compare your productivity in different time periods?

2. Have you and a friend ever deliberately taken two routes simultaneously to the same destination to see which was the faster route?

3. Do you frequently set deadlines with yourself for accomplishing certain tasks? (I will finish painting this wall by 2:00 p.m., I will clean out the garage by next Monday, etc.).

4. Are these deadlines, in retrospect, rather impossible to fullfil?

5. Do you make a study of which line at the bank or which checkout station at the supermarket is apt to be the quickest?

6. Are you impatient when slow drivers invade the fast, left lanes on the freeway?

7. When you take a vacation, do you like to make your time count, to see what there is to see, do what there is to do, or are you willing to sleep late some mornings at your hotel?

8. How long does it take you to drive home from work at night? Do you know the travel times for other hours of the day?

9. Are you infuriated when people keep you waiting and you have nothing to do with your time? Do you possibly take a book with you for such a possibility?

10. Do you ever use the phrases "Time is money," "Time is running out," or "Time's on my side"?

11. If you have a few minutes to wait in a reception area, do you sit back in the chair and read a magazine? Or are you apt to sit on the edge of the chair in expectation of being called

soon? An upholsterer at Mt. Zion Hospital in San Francisco noticed that he often had to replace the front edges of the chairs in the cardiology waiting room rather than the whole seats, as in the other reception areas.

12. Are you willing to wait in line to see a very special movie?

13. Do you usually finish your meal before the rest of the family?

Galen was possibly the first person to describe the cancer-prone personality when, twenty-five centuries ago, he noted that melancholic women are more apt to get cancer than sanguine (or happy) women. Simonton has observed the following personality characteristics of cancer patients:

1. A great tendency to hold resentment and a marked inability to forgive.
2. A tendency towards self-pity.
3. A poor ability to develop and maintain meaningful, long-term relationships.
4. A very poor self-image.

Additionally, the patient often feels that he has been rejected by either one or both of his parents.

Probably the most active investigator of the cancer-prone personality is Dr. Lawrence Le Shan.

He describes a person who (1) is unable to express anger, especially in his own defense; (2) feels unworthy and dislikes himself; (3) is tense over the relationship with one or both parents, and (4) experiences a severe emotional loss to which he reacts with the feelings of helplessness, hopelessness, isolation, and depression, which characterized his childhood period of emotional deprivation. In the typical pattern, cancer is diagnosed six months to a year later and, unless he does something to change the helpless-hopeless pattern, the outlook is not good. I sincerely hope that this does not describe you or anyone you love.

The opinion that things are "hopeless" and that you are "helpless" is a decision that you arrive at in your head and, therefore, one that you can change. Norman Cousins refused to view his critical illness as hopeless and, rather than feeling helpless, he helped to create a new treatment program for himself. Back in the days of polio epidemics, I noticed that some of the patients who recovered the use of their muscles had been initially more seriously afflicted than patients who didn't recover; the difference seemed to be that the first group didn't give up and label themselves "paralyzed." Stephan Pálos, the author of *The Chinese Art of Healing,* was a student of Chinese medicine in Budapest. When Hungary made its political break with the Peoples Republic of China, Pálos was arrested and put into solitary confinement for eight years. Instead of feeling helpless or hopeless, he used the time to practice his meditation and *asanas,* and outlined the principles of Chinese healing in his head. He feels he owes his present skill as a practitioner to the many years he spent in prison.

The best way not to feel helpless-hopeless is to practice coping with the many small dilemmas on the way to the bigger ones life will bring you. Instead of throwing up your hands in despair and walking away from a seemingly irreconcilable disagreement, see if there is some new way you can approach the conflict to achieve understanding. (Go to someone for marital counseling, perhaps.) If you have twenty problems to solve in an arithmetic exam and get stuck on the tenth one, don't feel hopeless. Skip it, go on to the next ones; then go back to the sticky one at the end if you have any time left. If the world seemingly doesn't like or want to buy your artistic product, keep trying. E.B. White, the writer who became so closely identified with the *New Yorker* magazine, submitted samples of his work twenty-two times before that magazine accepted any!

By all means, acknowledge to yourself all those times that were difficult for you, but where you persisted anyway and managed to cope. Think back to the incidents you remembered in the Glory-Brag exercise in Chapter 5. How many of them were situations in which you were tempted to give up but kept on trying? Give yourself some praise for all those times you learned to cope . . . the time the grease caught on fire and you put it out . . . the time you figured out where the lost car keys must be . . . the time your pet dog died and you learned how to deal with grief.

One technique for learning to reverse the helpless-hopeless thinking is a form of self-hypnosis called Autogenic Therapy. This was developed in Germany after the turn of the century, has been used widely in Europe, and is only now coming into popular acceptance in the United States. You first learn to relax by training with a set of formulae that you concentrate on for a minute or two each. (Do this while lying down with your eyes closed.)

1. I'm calm, I'm at peace.
2. My right arm is heavy. (Left-handed people use the left arm.)
3. My right arm is warm.
4. My pulse is calm and strong.
5. My breath is peaceful and regular. "It breathes me."
6. My solar plexus is warm.
7. My forehead is pleasantly cool.

Once relaxed, you then concentrate on an "intentional formula" designed for your particular need. To counteract feeling helpless, you might use the formula, "I am now able to cope with any emergency or any loss." Or, "I know what it is I need to do." What intentional formula would fit best for you?

When you are ready to end your session, use the formula: I'm alert and relaxed.

One way to learn to do autogenic therapy is to participate in a day-long workshop. Or, read a book and practice doing the formulae with a friend. Other intentional formulae that you might find useful:

I am now able to believe in my abilities.

I am now able to eat moderately.

I am now more and more able to initiate actions.

I am now able to express the full intensity of my feelings.

I am now able to acknowledge my wisdom.

One final thought before we end this chapter: There is an excellent book that describes the workings of your body in detail and in an interesting fashion. It suggests which illnesses you can treat yourself and how; which symptoms call for the cooperation of a physician; and what you can do to prevent illness. One of the most valuable parts is the visualization exercise for the creation of your own imaginary physician, an ancient exercise that has been revived recently by Silva Mind Control and some of the other mental training groups. The book is aptly entitled *The Well Body Book*, and the authors are Mike Samuels, M.D., and Hal Bennett.

CHAPTER 10

DEATH (AND THE POSSIBILITY THAT YOU'RE IN CHARGE HERE, TOO!)

> No one knows whether death may not turn out to be the greatest of blessings for a human being; and yet people fear it as if they knew for certain that it is the greatest of evils.
>
> —Socrates

DEATH . . . Stop a minute and acknowledge your reaction to this word. Is this a subject that you fear? Do you spend a fair portion of your present time ruminating about the future death of yourself or of people you love?

Or perhaps you believe that this is an unknowable subject and therefore you refuse to give it any time or thought. In this case, do you find yourself attempting to change the subject or leaving the group when death becomes a topic of conversation?

These two attitudes—fear of death or denial of death—seem to underlie many of the problems in the people who come to see me. There was Peggy, who was afraid to go too far away from her house or to cross a bridge. And Harry, who hastened to sample all new foods, visit all new countries, and become sexually involved with all new women. And Millie, who complained of a generalized unhappiness although she seemingly had everything a person would want. Once they had dealt with the fact of their own inevitable deaths and found some meaning for their living and dying, the intitial "problems" seemed to take care of themselves.

194

As a result, I've come to believe that it is of crucial importance for each one of us to come to grips with the fact that we will someday die and to take charge of our thoughts about this. What you believe about death seems to determine how you live your life.

Death Exercise I

Get into comfortable position with your spine erect.

Take several Complete Breaths.

Now go back in your imagination to your youngest years. When did you first learn that animals die? That people die?

See if you can recall the exact circumstances in which you made this discovery. Be back there again. Observe the reactions of any other people in the drama—the adults, the children. What are you feeling?

When did you first know someone who died? Recall that event and your feelings about it in full detail. What did you think happened to that person after death? Be back there again. What are you feeling?

When did you first realize that you, too, would die some day? How did you feel about that realization? How do you feel about it now?

This first experience with death (or the knowledge of death) often exerts a powerful imprinting on the mind and emotions of people. If the adults are frightened and crying about a loved one's death, then the child perceives death as something bad and to be feared. If the child's first knowledge of death is derived from his parents' overprotectiveness of his health, then he may become fearful and overly concerned about his own dying. Jill's introduction was a more fortunate one. When she was eight, her grandfather, who had been paralyzed for a year from a stroke, died of a second stroke. Her mother, in giving Jill the news, compared his dying to the emergence of a butterfly from its cocoon.

Another way to ferret out your possibly hidden attitudes and feelings about death:

Drawing Death

Get a pad of drawing paper and some oil pastels or crayons or felt-tipped pens or whatever.

Close your eyes.

Take several Complete Breaths.

Now select a color and start drawing your concept of death. Don't consciously choose a symbol. Just start drawing. (If this is difficult for you, then take the crayon or pen in your nondominant hand . . . which would be the left hand for right-handed people.) If you feel like writing words, then write words.

When you feel finished, take a new piece of paper (and possibly a different color) and start drawing your *feelings* about death. Again, try to do this spontaneously without thinking about what you are doing.

When you feel finished, put both sheets of paper aside. Come back to them at a later time and see what you see.

It's interesting to notice the different colors people choose. For many people, death is black (many Americans are acculturated to think black . . . black clothing, black hearses). Others choose ivory, pale yellow, gold, green, rose, and so on.

People have chosen symbols ranging from the Grim Reaper and the black-cloaked stranger of Ingmar Bergman's *The Seventh Seal* to rainbows, butterflies, and evanescent clouds. There is a similar diversity in the ways in which people draw their feelings about death. I don't want to give any more examples here that might influence what you draw.

Here's a final exercise on death which is the most important one of all:

Death Exercise II

Sit with your spine erect. Close your eyes.

Take several Complete Breaths.

Visualize on the wall in front of you a large number that is the same number as your current age.

Click! The digital readout is one number greater.

Click! One year more.

Click! One year more. And so on until you reach the number that is the age at which you imagine you will die.

Imagine that you are waking up on the morning of what will be your last day alive. Where are you? How are you feeling? What do you feel in your body?

Are you ill? Or will death come as the result of an accident? If you are ill, do you know that you are dying?

Proceed in your imagination through the events of this last day. Are there people with you? Who? How do they feel about you? How do you feel about them?

If you are aware of your dying, is there a death poem that you would like to write? Or any feelings or thoughts that you would like to share with anyone?

Now imagine the actual moment of your death. What do you experience?

Now imagine the moments after your death. What do you experience?

When you have finished this exercise, write a full description of all that you imagined and felt. Remind yourself that this is a deliberate fantasy that you have created and you do *not* have to stay with this program.

Your life does not have to end in the manner or at the age that you have just fantasized.

This exercise is important because it can help you to discover unconscious fantasies that you may have developed about the manner and time of your death. Do you perhaps expect to die of a heart attack at forty-five, just like your same-sex parent? Linda developed a heart murmur when she was one year younger than the age at which her mother had had a fatal heart attack. She did not get better until she uncovered her hidden fantasy that she would die at the same age that her mother had died. Only then was she able to realize that she had created the fantasy and that she could substitute a long-life fantasy instead if she wished. She did so wish, and additionally stopped smoking and adopted an exercise regime to implement her new expectation.

Fred realized that he was expecting to die a violent death at a young age and had actively courted that death with his car racing and rock climbing. Other people have fantasized a peaceful death of old age with no illness and no pain, surrounded by loving children and grandchildren. Energy follows thought, so that the death that you anticipate for yourself may very well happen according to your schedule and your blueprint.

What kind of death do you imagine for yourself? You may not have a special time set aside for the development of this fantasy, as did Bob in the example of the Freeway Blanking Out Syndrome, but I feel sure that you do have *some* fantasy on the topic.

> It is not death that is the source of all man's evils, but rather the fear of death.
>
> —Epictetus

The fears that people have about death are many. Some fear they will have a painful and protracted illness. Some fear they will be old and abandoned and left to die alone. Some fear that they will die before they have accomplished the goals they have set for themselves. Others rage at the lack of control they have over the time of their death (with a few of these taking back that control from Fate and committing suicide). The most pervasive fear seems to be the fear of loss of identity, the ending of one's personality.

In the latter part of the last exercise, did you fantasize a life after death and a continuation of your consciousness in some form? Or did you imagine that death was the end, lights out, complete darkness? Those people who believe that death is extinction have, understandably, the greatest fears of dying.

Life after "Death"

There is a growing body of circumstantial evidence that is strongly suggestive of a life after death. Interestingly, these reports bear a striking similarity to descriptions of the afterworld given by Eastern religions.

Dr. Raymond Moody has collected the reports of more than 150 people who either nearly died or who experienced actual clinical death and were resuscitated. All of them report experiences of an after-death existence. Typically the "dead" person is greeted by spirits of departed friends and relatives who come to help him in his transition. A being of light appears who gives him an instant re-run of the major events of his life and asks him to evaluate his time on earth. For various reasons, the dead person decides to return to life in his body. It's a difficult decision to make, as he is feeling immensely joyful, peaceful, and loving in his new state.

Moody's respondents typically returned with the feeling that they had tasks still to do in this world or work to complete as a result of their glimpse of the after-world. "I've got quite a lot of changing to do before I leave here," said one man.

Check now to see what are you thinking and feeling. Are you scoffing? ("Where's your proof?") Or are you feeling that this makes sense and you wish that you could believe that this is what really happens?

See what your response is to the following fantasy exercise:

Fantasy of a Brook

Sit with your spine erect.

Take several Complete Breaths.

Imagine that you are climbing a mountain trail that has a small brook flowing next to it.

When the trail and the brook part company, leave the trail and follow the course of the stream to its source . . . a few drops of water bubbling up from a spring in the ground.

Now imagine that you *are* those few drops of water. Feel yourself trickling down the slope, joining with other trickles to become a brook, and then joining with other brooks to become a wide stream. Notice how slowly you flow where the land is almost flat and how rapidly you move where it is steep. How do you feel about the rocks that lie in your path? And the fish that swim in your depths?

Now you have become a very wide river and are moving more slowly . . . sometimes through cities, sometimes through the countryside. How do you feel about the boats and ships and people on your surface?

Now as you near the ocean, some of the salty seawater becomes combined with you. And now you are entering the ocean and becoming a part of it, your pure original spring water indistinguishable from the rest.

Imagine yourself being a wave that crests and then flings itself toward the shore. Be the part of the wave that creeps the highest onto the sand, clings a moment, and then pulls itself away to rejoin the ocean.

Imagine yourself being a still part of the ocean many fathoms deep in the dark.

Imagine yourself being a huge wave in the center of the ocean. Be one of the drops of the crest of the wave that is wafted from the crest and becomes vapor, going to join a cloud of vapor drops that is traveling slowly. Now over the ocean. Now over the coast. Now over the foothills. Now over a high mountain range.

Now imagine that you are part of the rain released from that cloud. You fall gently on the mountain, sinking into the soil, becoming part of a spring that bubbles up from the ground. As you trickle down the mountainside, realize that you are becoming a brook again in the same place where you were a brook once before.

Whatever your belief system is about death and the hereafter, the really important questions are:

Who am I?

For what purpose am I here?

Wise Old Person Exercise

Sit with spine erect.

Take several Complete Breaths.

Imagine that you are exploring a large, old Victorian house that is currently unoccupied.

Go through each of the rooms, noticing the old furniture, lamps, paintings, embroidery.

Climb the stairs and prowl through the bedrooms on the second floor.

And now you notice a velvet curtain that is partially concealing a door. Pull the curtain aside and open the door. Now you see a stairway that, judging by the dust on the steps, has not been used for a long time.

Climb the stairs and open the door at the top of the steps.

Now you find yourself in a book-lined room that is flooded with light from all sides and a skylight above. You are starting to read some of the book titles when you realize that sitting in one corner of the room is a very old person.

This person says, "I've been expecting you." You realize that this person has all knowledge and will answer any questions you ask.

Ask now: What is the purpose for which I was born?

Listen to the answer and ask any other questions that you wish. Thank your wise old person and go back down the stairs and leave the house.

When you finish this exercise, write about it in your journal. The "wise old person" is, of course, the hidden wisdom in each of us. Many of us are hesitant to acknowledge our own inner wisdom so we project it onto others.

Years of Retirement

We can be thankful for the fact of death; it is the event that causes us to search for the meaning of life. With the advances in medicine, sanitation, and disease control in the past hundred years, we are seeing many more people live longer lives. It's common for some to live ten or twenty years after they have retired from their working careers. This is a marvelous gift of extra time to look inward. An elderly person has a choice. He can use this time to make contact with his Self and to see if he feels he has accomplished his assigned tasks for this lifetime. Or she can run from this contemplation and focus on the frailties of her aging body. Unfortunately, the hottest topics of conversation in some retirement communities are illnesses, medications, and doctors.

What is your plan for your retirement years?

Old Age Reflection Exercise

Imagine that you are a very old person and are looking back on the life you have lived.

What is *the* most important thing about you that you'd like your friends and your family and the world to know about you after you're gone?

What about you has *made a difference?*

Write in your journal about it.

The Art of Dying

Tibetan Buddhists believe that death can be the moment of spiritual liberation for those who remain conscious, clear-headed, and calm—rather than confused and fearful. Their classic manual on how to die, *The Tibetan Book of the Dead*, describes the periods before and after death as a series of *bardos*; and each *bardo* offers different challenges to the soul on its way to enlightenment. All need to be met with calm and clarity and a recognition that all the terrors are simply projections of one's own mind.

If this be true, then those individuals who have been practicing the art of self-observation and know well the content of their minds will be better prepared for the journey through the *bardos* than many of us. One rare individual in our culture who had an understanding of the value of being conscious at the hour of death was Aldous Huxley. In his novel *Island*, the old grandmother is kept conscious by her husband, who holds her and croons, "My little love, . . . now you can let go, my darling. Now you can let go. Let go. Let go of this poor old body. You don't need it any more. Let it fall away from you. Leave it lying here like a pile of wornout clothes . . . Go on, my darling, go on into the Light, into the peace, into the living peace of the Clear Light."

A decade after this book was published, Huxley would himself die in full awareness, with his wife, Laura, saying to him many phrases similar to those in *Island*: "Light and free and let go, darling; . . . you are going toward the light. Willingly and consciously . . . you are are going forward and up." He had asked for and received a shot of LSD (similar to the *moksha* medicine in *Island*) to assist him in making an aware transition.

There is a classic Buddhist parable about a traveler who is chased by a tiger to the edge of a cliff. There the traveler seizes a thick vine and swings himself over the edge, only to discover that there is another tiger snarling in wait for him at the bottom of the cliff. There he is, suspended midway between the two tigers, when two mice begin gnawing away at his vine. He realizes that his lifebelt will soon be cut through. Then he notices a wild strawberry growing just within reach. He picks it and savors its delicious flavor.

This illustrates the Eastern philosophy of remaining conscious and *in the present* at the time of death, not letting your Critic berate you for having taken a road where there are apt to be tigers, and not speculating about what lies ahead. Just tasting the strawberry. As Ram Dass says, "The game is to stay fully conscious at the moment of death . . . Otherwise you can get caught in the pain or melodrama of the fear of ceasing to be who you thought you were." So the art of dying can be seen as an extension of the art of living—staying alert and aware of what is happening *right now*.

When it comes to be your time to die, my wish for you is that you will let go, let go of past and future, and flow into the next moment as if you were returning to the source of all true love. Whether this is "true" or not, for me it beats going out kicking and screaming and trying to hang onto an obsolete body.

The Hospice Movement

It's not too easy for the dying person to remain alert if he is oversedated for pain relief, as is the practice of many physicians and the custom in many hospitals. St. Christopher's Hospice in London uses a medication called Brompton's mixture,* which relieves the symptoms and intractable pain of terminal cancer while permitting the patient to remain conscious and alert.

St. Christopher's and its director, Dr. Cicely Saunders, have been the innovators in a rapidly growing humanistic approach to the care of the dying. The word "hospice" comes from the inns of the Middle Ages that were established to offer a resting place for those travelers making a pilgrimage to the Holy Land. The twentieth-century hospice is providing a place for the terminally ill to ease their deaths. Stoddard reports that each person is seen and treated as an individual and is ministered to—physically, psychologically, and spiritually. There are no fixed visiting hours as in the traditional hospital; visits from family, friends, children, and even pets are encouraged. The atmosphere is light and loving, with a ratio of greater than one staff member per patient. The staff, partially volunteer in most hospices, report

---

*It contains heroin, cocaine, alcohol, syrup and chloroform water and is taken orally every four hours. To conform with USA narcotics laws the Methodist Hospital of Indiana has modified the formula as follows: Morphine 10 mg, cocaine 10 mg, Aromatic Elixir (orange oil, lemon oil, coriander oil, anise oil and 22% alcohol) 20 ml.

that caring for the dying is a rewarding and exhilarating expenditure of their time rather than a morbid task. The dying person is given a sense of closeness to others, someone to listen, someone to hold a hand, someone to talk to about the meaning of life and death.

Bereavement and Grief

> Blessed are those who mourn:
> for they shall be comforted.

The period after the death of a loved one is typically a time of tremendous emotional upheaval. The first stage is usually that of shock, in which you will momentarily forget the new reality and have to remind yourself of what has happened. The world may seem unreal, and you may go through the customary rituals and rigors mechanically and seemingly without feeling.

The next stage is the suffering of grief. There may be anger and rage at the one who has died. There may be feelings of guilt—probably to the extent that there was unexpressed resentment for the dead person while alive. There can be self-torture trips: "If-Only-I-had" and the Sentimental Memory game are two common ones at this juncture. If you have a well-developed Victim subpersonality, you may enjoy feeling victimized by this death.

The length and pain of this stage can be lessened if you take care of as much of your emotional unfinished business as possible with your Important Other before death intervenes. The end of grief can be accelerated by active mourning; by being very conscious of your thoughts and feelings and choosing to share them with some caring Others. Unfortunately, the clergy are frequently not equipped to be of much help to the mourners; bereaved writers such as Joyce Phipps report that people who have previously gone through their own bereavements are better sources of comfort. You can later cement the third, or recovery, stage of your bereavement by extending similar understanding, empathy, love, and comfort to some newly bereaved people.

Most important is the acknowledgment that in grieving for a loved one you are clinging to the idea of permanence, of "security." Epictetus reminds us that those we love are mortal; we have·them with us for the appointed season, and "if you long for your friend, or your son, when you cannot have them, you are wishing for figs in winter."

In working through your grief you can make progress in your own growth as a person. You may very well find that your love for the dead person becomes more clarified and purer. As Kahlil Gibran said, "That which you love most [in your friend] may be clearer in his absence, as the mountain to the climber is clearer from the plain."

Ultimately the grieving person will be able to say "goodbye" to the dead one. This does not mean a total eclipse of past memories, nor a refusal to entertain thoughts and feelings about the person. It means a clear acknowledgment that this phase of your association with your dead loved one is finished, and a willingness to grow and to experiment with new ways of being has taken its place.

What have you been feeling and thinking as you were reading this section? Have you had a Significant Other die recently? Are you still grieving? If so, what part of you is hanging on to memories, unwilling to say "goodbye"?

Suicide

Suicide is a possibility that probably everyone over the age of twelve (and an astonishingly large number under twelve) has contemplated. It is a way in which about one hundred Americans die every day.

There are so many different kinds of suicide and so many ramifications. There is the suicide-threat-that-fails and becomes a real death. Here the person is possibly trying to control his or her Significant Other and the suicide can be seen as a very hostile act.

At the opposite end of the spectrum are altruistic suicides by people who are terminally ill and wish to save their families emotional pain and to conserve the family finances from the inroads of expensive medical and hospital bills. Or there is the heroic suicide, such as that of the resistance fighter who kills himself at the point of capture to avoid the torture in which he might betray his comrades.

A common denominator of most other suicides seems to be a feeling of total loneliness and the lack of any close, nurturing relationships.

I'd like for you to stop here and see if you remember any times when you seriously considered killing yourself.

What were the reasons?

Did you go as far as planning your method?

Did you ever write a suicide note, either on paper or in your head?

If so, take a few minutes to reflect on what happened afterwards. Notice all the things you would have missed out on in the years following if you had actually done it.

I seriously considered killing myself when I was eleven. My mother had had a nervous breakdown and was in a sanitarium in another state. I was living with my newly-met grandfather (whom I adored) in a culture completely different from the one in which I had spent my first ten years. Then my grandfather died. I had not been allowed to visit him in the hospital, and I sank into feelings of hopeless, helpless despondency about my living situation. If I had been more knowledgeable about methods of suicide, I might really have done it. The only means at my disposal was a poison that I was afraid might not work and I was sure would hurt. Fortunately, other relatives rescued me rather quickly. My mother recovered from her nervous breakdown, and we were able to live together again. I would certainly hate to have missed out on the rich, funny, sad, happy, and exciting times since then.

According to Dr. Moody, the near-death experiences of those he interviewed who had attempted suicide were uniformly characterized as being unpleasant—in sharp contrast to those of patients who nearly died from an illness. They seemed to go to an unpleasant "limbo" place where they felt they would be staying for a long time. This seemed to be a penalty for having attempted a premature release before having fulfilled life's assignment. A man who shot himself and was resuscitated after the natural death of his wife said: "I didn't go where (my wife) was. I went to an awful place . . . I immediately saw what a mistake I had made . . . I thought, 'I wish I hadn't done it.'"

Reflect on your own thinking. What is it that stops you from taking your own life? Albert Camus said that there is only one philosophical question worth discussing and that is whether to say "yes" or "no" to life, whether to live or to commit suicide. And this is a choice that each of us makes every day.

Two Sides of the Coin: Life and Death

I'd like to end with a fantasy exercise that is partially responsible for this book being written:

The Next Three Years[*]

Become aware of your breathing . . . your breath going in and your breath coming out . . . notice what parts of your body move as you breathe . . . notice what parts of your body are in contact with the chair, floor, bed, or whatever . . . Allow yourself to yield to the chair, the floor, to let them support you.

Imagine that you have been told that you have just three years left to live. You will be in good health for these years . . . What was your immediate response? . . . To start planning how you would spend your time? Or to be angry at how short the time is?

Rather than "raging against the dying of the light" or getting bogged down in the mechanics of how you die in this fantasy, decide how you want to spend your time, *how you want to live these last three years.*

Where do you want to live?
With whom do you want to live?
Do you want to work?
To study?

After you have finished this fantasy, compare this life you have planned with the life you are living now.
How are they the same?
How are they different?
Are there any ingredients from your fantasy life that you would like to incorporate into your current life?

---

[*] This exercise is a modification of one of Alan Lakein's three "lifetime questions."

Now realize that the assumption that you would die in three years is only a fantasy for the purpose of this exercise. Put that thought away from you. And keep from the fantasy only what seems to fit for you and that you want to hold onto. Write down whatever happened that seems significant to you.

This exercise has been very useful to many people in helping them become aware of what they really want to do, how they really want to live their lives. They become aware of which people they cherish (and decide to spend more time with them as a result). Or they become acutely aware that they are wasting their lives in an unpleasant job or in distasteful surroundings. Or that school is solely a means to an end and affords no current nourishment.

I had done this exercise many times before doing it again with my Wednesday group in June, 1975. I had been "talking about" writing a book for several years but had written only a dozen or so miscellaneous and unconnected pages. In doing the exercise I felt a very clear need not to die without having put on paper in even an elementary way some of the things that I had learned so far in working with people. These feelings catalyzed me into action, and I started working seriously on the book you are reading now.

Are there any actions that you feel similarly mobilized to do with the knowledge that the length of your life is limited?

The End and Goodbye

And so, as we each will one day come to the end of life in our present physical forms, we come to the end of this journey, I as writer and you as reader of this book. It's been an important process for me, and I hope it has been useful for you as well. I'm feeling the lack of response now as I finish and would welcome feedback from any who care to give it about your own personal work as you've read the book. You can reach me by writing to the publisher.

Stay aware!

BIBLIOGRAPHY

Chapter One

Beisser, A. "The Paradoxical Theory of Change," in Fagan, J. and Shepherd, I.L., *Gestalt Therapy Now*. Palo Alto, Cal.: Science and Behavior Books, 1970.

Chapter Two

Assagioli, R. *Psychosynthesis*. New York: Viking, 1971.
Gerbner, G. and Gross, L. "The Scary World of TV's Heavy Viewer." *Psychology Today*, April, 1976.
Hanh, T.N. *The Miracle of Mindfulness*. Boston: Beacon Press, 1976.
Huxley, A. *Island*. New York: Harper and Row, 1962.
Krishnamurti, J. *The First and Last Freedom*. New York: Harper and Row, 1954.
Maslow, A. *Toward a Psychology of Being*. Cincinnati: Van Nostrand, 1962.
Merton, R.M. *Social Theory and Social Structure*. Glencoe, Ill: Free Press, 1957.
Ouspensky, P.D. *In Search of the Miraculous*. New York: Harcourt, Brace & World, 1949.
Perls, F. *Gestalt Therapy Verbatim*. Lafayette, Cal.: Real People Press, 1969.
Thurber, J. "The Secret Life of Walter Mitty," in *My World and Welcome to It*. New York: Harcourt, 1942.
Vargiu, J.G. "Subpersonalities," in *Synthesis*, Vol. 1, 1974.
Yeomans, T. "The Pie, a Psychosynthesis Exercise," in *Synthesis*, Vol. 1, 1974.

Chapter Three

Bonforte, J. *The Philosophy of Epictetus*. New York: Philosophical Library, 1955.
Brecher, R. and Brecher, E. *An Analysis of Human Sexual Response*. New York: Signet, 1966.
Cuber, J., and Harroff, P. *Sex and the Significant Americans*. New York: Pelican, 1965.
Fromm, E. *The Art of Loving*. New York: Harper and Row, 1956.
Greene, G. *Blue Skies, No Candy*. New York: William Morrow, 1976.
Greer, G. *The Female Eunuch*. New York: McGraw Hill, 1971.
Kramer, J. *The Passionate Mind: A Manual for Living Creatively with One's Self*. Millbrae, Cal.: Celestial Arts, 1974.

Masters, W.M., and Johnson, V. *Human Sexual Response*. Boston: Little, Brown, 1966.

Mood, J.L.L. *Rilke on Love and Other Difficulties*. New York: W.W. Norton, 1975.

Previn, D. "Mythical Kings and Iguanas." Mediarts Music, Inc., 1971.

Rajneesh, B.S. *The Book of the Secrets*, Vol. 1. New York: Harper and Row, 1974.

Satir, V. *Peoplemaking*. Palo Alto, Cal.: Science and Behavior Books, 1972.

Sherfey, M.J. *The Nature and Evolution of Female Sexuality*. New York: Random House, 1966.

Chapter Four

Jong, E. *Fear of Flying*. New York: Holt, Rinehart and Winston, 1973.

Nin. A. *The Diary of Anais Nin, 1931–1934*, New York: Harcourt, Brace & World, 1966.

_____. *The Diary of Anais Nin, 1934–1939*. New York: Harcourt, Brace & World, 1967.

_____. *Linotte, The Early Diary of Anais Nin, 1914–1920*. New York: Harcourt Brace Jovanovich, 1978.

Weingarten, V. *Intimations of Mortality*. New York: Alfred A. Knopf, 1978.

Chapter Five

The Center Magazine. "Gray Panther Power, an Interview with Maggie Kuhn." March/April, 1975.

Goldhurst, R. *Many are the Hearts: The Agony and the Triumph of Ulysses S. Grant*. New York: Readers' Digest-Crowell, 1975.

Hesse, H. "Childhood of the Magician," in *Autobiographical Writings*. New York: Farrar, Strauss and Giroux, 1972.

Jung, C.G. *Memories, Dreams, Reflections*. New York: Pantheon, 1961.

MANAS, Vol. 28, No. 40, October 1, 1975.

Perls, F. *In and Out the Garbage Pail*. Lafayette, Cal.: Real People Press, 1969.

Chapter Six

Bro, H.B. *Edgar Cayce on Dreams*. New York: Paperback Library, 1968.

de Becker, R. *The Understanding of Dreams and Their Influence on the History of Man*. London: George Allen and Unwin, 1968.

Dement, W.G. *Some Must Watch While Some Must Sleep*. San Francisco: W.H. Freeman, 1974.

Faraday, A. *The Dream Game*. New York: Harper and Row, 1974.

Freud, S. *The Interpretation of Dreams*, London: George Allen and Unwin, 1961 (originally published 1900.)

Garfield, P. *Creative Dreaming*. New York: Ballantine Books, 1976.

Gerard, R.W. "The Biological Basis of Imagination," in Ghiselin, B., Editor, *The Creative Process*. New York: Mentor Books, 1955.

Goodenough, D.R., Shapiro, A., Holden, M., and Steinschiber, L. "A Comparison of 'Dreamers' and 'Nondreamers'," *Journal of Abnormal and Social Psychology*, Vol. 62, 1959.

Green, C. *Lucid Dreams*. London: Institute of Psychophysical Research, 1968.

Hadfield, J.A. *Dreams and Nightmares*. Baltimore: Penguin, 1954.

Jenks, K. *Journey of a Dream Animal*. New York: Pocket Books, 1977.

Jung, C.G. "The Archetype and the Collective Unconscious," in *Collected Works*, Vol. 9. Princeton, N.J.: Bollingen, 1968.

_____. "Two Essays on Analytical Psychology," in *Collected Works*, Vol. 7. Princeton, N.J.: Bollingen, 1966.

Perls, F. *Gestalt Therapy Verbatim*. Lafayette, Cal.: Real People Press, 1969.

Reed, H. "Dream Incubation: A Reconstruction of a Ritual Contemporary Form." *Journal of Humanistic Psychology*, V. 16, No. 4, Fall, 1976.

Stewart, K. "Dream Theory in Malaya," in Tart, C.T., Editor, *Altered States of Consciousness*. New York: John Wiley, 1969.

Tart, C.T. "'High Dream': New State of Consciousness," in Tart, Editor, *Altered States of Consciousness*. New York: John Wiley, 1969.

van der Post, L. *Jung and the Story of Our Time*. New York: Pantheon Books, 1975.

Van Eeden, F. "A Study of Dreams," in Tart, C.T., Editor, *Altered States of Consciousness*. New York: John Wiley, 1969.

Chapter Seven

Dass, R. *The Only Dance There Is*. Garden City, N.Y.: Anchor, 1974.

Hanh, T.N. *The Miracle of Mindfulness*. Boston: Beacon Press, 1976.

Herrigel, E. *Zen in the Art of Archery*. New York: Vintage Books, 1971.

Humphreys, C. *Concentration and Meditation*. Baltimore: Penguin, 1970.

Joy, W.B. *Joy's Way*. Los Angeles: J.P. Tarcher, 1979.

LeShan, L. *How to Meditate*. New York: Bantam Books, 1975.

Osborn, A., Editor, *The Teachings of Ramana Maharshi*. New York: Samuel Weiser, 1962.

Rajneesh, B.S. *Meditation: The Art of Ecstasy*. New York: Harper Colophon, 1976.

Roof, S. "What is Meditation?", in Hanson, V., Editor, *Approaches to Meditation*. Wheaton, Ill.: Theosophical, 1973.
von Dürckheim, K. *Daily Life as Spiritual Exercise: The Way of Transformation*. New York: Perennial Library, 1972.

Chapter Eight

Schachtel, E. *Metamorphosis*. New York: Basic Books, 1959.
Wilde, O. *De Profundis and Other Writings*. Harmondsworth: Penguin, 1973.

Chapter Nine

Airola, P. *How to Get Well*. Phoenix, Arizona: Health Plus Publishers, 1974.
Blair, G. "Why Dick Can't Stop Smoking: The Politics Behind Our National Addiction," *Mother Jones*, January, 1979, 31–42.
Brown, B. *New Mind, New Body*. New York: Harper and Row, 1974.
Cheraskin, E., and Ringsdorf, W.M., Jr., with Brecher, A. *Psychodietetics: Food as the Key to Emotional Health*. Briarcliff Manor, N.Y.: Stein and Day, 1974.
Cooper, K.H. *The New Aerobics*. New York: Bantam, 1970.
Cousins, N. "Anatomy of an Illness as Perceived by the Patient," *New England Journal of Medicine*. Vol. 295, No. 26, 1458–63 (1976).
Davis, A. *Let's Get Well*. New York: Harcourt, Brace & World, 1965.
Dement, W.G. *Some Must Watch While Some Must Sleep*. San Francisco: W.H. Freeman, 1974.
Dufty, W. *Sugar Blues*. New York: Warner Books, 1975.
Friedman, M., and Rosenman, R.H. *Type A Behavior and Your Heart*. New York: Alfred A. Knopf, 1974.
Holmes, T.H. and Rahe, R.H. "The Social Readjustment Rating Scale," *Journal of Psychosomatic Research*, Vol. 11, 1967, 213–218.
Jones, H.B. *Sensual Drugs*. Cambridge University Press, 1977.
LeShan, L. "A basic psychological orientation apparently associated with malignant disease." *Psychiatric Quarterly*, 36 (1961): 314–30.
LeShan, L. and Worthington, R.E. "Some recurrent life history patterns observed in patients with malignant disease." *Journal of Nervous and Mental Disease*, 124 (1956): 460–65.
Lidz, T. "General Concepts of Psychosomatic Medicine." In Arieti, S., Editor, *American Handbook of Psychiatry*. New York: Basic Books, 1959.
Miller, D.E. *Bodymind: The Whole Person Health Book*. New York: Pinnacle, 1975.
Pálos, S. *The Chinese Art of Healing*. New York: Bantam, 1972.
Ramacharaka. *Science of Breath*. Chicago: Yogi Publication Society, 1904.

Samuels, M., and Bennett, H. *The Well Body Book*. New York: Random House, 1973.

Schultz, J., and Luthe, W. *Autogenic Training: A Psychophysiologic Approach in Psychotherapy*. New York: Grune and Stratton, 1959.

Selye, H. *The Stress of Life*. New York: McGraw Hill, 1956.

_____. *Stress without Distress*. New York: J.P. Lippincott, 1974.

Simeons, A.T.W. *Man's Presumptuous Brain*. New York: E.P. Dutton, 1961.

Simonton, O.C., and Simonton, S.S. "Belief systems and management of the emotional aspects of malignancy," *Journal of Transpersonal Psychology*, 1975, 29–47.

Simonton, O.C., Mathews-Simonton, S., and Creighton, J. *Getting Well Again*. Los Angeles: J.P. Tarcher, 1978.

Chapter Ten

Assagioli, R. *The Act of Will*. New York: Viking, 1973.

Bonforte, J. *The Philosophy of Epictetus*. New York: Philosophical Library, 1955.

Camus, A. *The Myth of Sisyphus*. New York: Alfred A. Knopf, 1955.

Dass, R. "Talk at the San Francisco Gestalt Institute," in Downing, J., Editor, *Gestalt Awareness*. New York: Harper and Row—Perennial, 1976.

Fremantle, F., and Trungpa, C. *Tibetan Book of the Dead*. Boulder, Colorado: Shambhala, 1975.

Gibran, K. *The Prophet*. New York: Alfred A. Knopf, 1923.

Huxley, A. *Island*. New York: Harper and Row, 1962.

Huxley, L.A. *This Timeless Moment, A Personal View of Aldous Huxley*. Millbrae, Cal.: Celestial Arts, 1975.

Humma, K.G. and others. *A Primer on Brompton's Cocktail*. Indianapolis, Ind.: Methodist Hospital of Indiana, Inc., (no date).

Lakein, A. *How to Get Control of Your Time and Your Life*. New York: Signet, 1974.

Moody, R.A. Jr. *Life after Life*. Atlanta: Mockingbird Books, 1975.

_____. *Reflections on Life after Life*. Covington, Georgia: Bantam/ Mockingbird, 1977.

Phipps, J. *Death's Single Privacy*. New York: Seabury Press, 1974.

Stoddard, S. *Hospice: Dying as the Experience of a Lifetime*. New York: Stein and Day, 1978.

Watts, A. *The Wisdom of Insecurity*. New York: Pantheon Books, 1951.

INDEX OF EXERCISES

Age Regression / 101
Anniversary / 110
"As-if" / 43
Asking for a Certain Dream / 130
Body Awareness / 157
Breath Awareness / 164
Chinese Temple / 148
Complete Breathing / 165
Cork on the Ocean / 43
Corrective Emotional
    Experience / 109
Death I / 195
Death II / 197
Defining Your Critic / 33
Dialogue with Absent Dream / 118
Dialogue with Time / 189
Dialogue with Your Overeating
    Subpersonality / 176
Disidentification / 38
Diversion / 16
Doughnut / 28
Doughnut Dialogue / 31
Drawing Death / 196
Dream Invention / 118
Eating with Mindfulness / 175
Energy Induction / 46
Evening Review / 23
Exercises / 2
Fairy Godmother / 61
Fantasy of a Brook / 200
Finishing an Interrupted
    Dream / 126
Glory-Brag / 113
Happiness Quotient I / 54
Happiness Quotient II / 55
House Plan Recall / 105
"I Appreciate" Game / 75
Ideal Future Contract / 70
Insomnia / 181

Intuition / 76
"I Resent" Game / 75
"I Want" Game / 74
Jealousy / 79
Lighthouse / 48
Meet Your Saboteur / 34
Movement Appraisal / 179
Next Three Years / 209
Nourishing the Child-That-
    You-Were / 108
Object-Centered Perception / 162
Old Age Reflection / 203
Putting Labels on Your
    Thoughts / 24
Recapitulation of Your Sexual
    History / 88
Reclaiming Your Irridescence / 147
Relaxation Prelude / 42
Reliving Past Positives / 44
Exercises / 3
Requests and Demands / 68
Rhythmic Breathing / 167
Satisfying Secret Needs / 72
Secret Garden / 47
Sensory Awareness / 152
Setting the Intention to Remember
    Your Dream / 117
Significant Other / 51
Smoking with Awareness / 178
Subpersonality Psychodrama / 32
Temple of Silence / 45
Twenty-four Hour Food and
    Drink Accounting / 169
Unconditional Love / 90
Visualization Demonstration / 40
Visualization for Complete
    Health / 187
Wise Old Person / 202
Working on Your Dream / 121

INDEX

Addictions, 177
Aerobics, 180
Affection, need for, 60–61, 84–85
Ain't-I-Awful, 19
Airola, Paavo, 172
Alcohol, 171, 180
Alcoholics Anonymous, 172
Anima, 135
Animus, 135
Ankylosing spondylitis, 188
Anniversary phenomenon, 110–11, 198
Approval, need for, 60–61, 87
Aramaic language, 91
Aserinsky, Eugene, 115
Assagioli, Roberto, 27, 37
Atom, model of conceived, 131
Autobiography, 99–114
Autogenic therapy, 192–93

Barbiturates, 116, 126, 182
Behavior patterns, obsolete, 36
Bennett, Hal, 193
Benzene molecule, structure of, 131
Bergman, Ingmar, 197
Berne, Eric, 27
Biofeedback, 184
Blue Skies, No Candy, 84
Body awareness, 150, 156–60
Bohr, Niels, 131
Breathing, 163–68
Br'er Rabbit Syndrome, 65
Brompton's mixture, 205
Buddha, 141, 142
Buddhism, 10, 26, 142, 144, 204

Caffeinism, 170, 173
Camus, Albert, 208
Cancer-prone personality, 191
Candid Camera, 188

Carbohydrates, refined, 170–71
Cayce, Edgar, 115
Change, 11–12
Cheraskin, Emanuel, 170, 172
Chicago, University of, 115
Childhood, traumatic events in, 36, 57, 108
Chinese Art of Healing (Pálos), 192
Chinese medicine, 163, 192
Coffee, 170
Coleridge, Samuel Taylor, 131
Collective unconscious, 133–34, 147
Collins, Mabel, 52
Communication games, 73–75
Comparison trips, 20, 77, 79, 80–84
Competition, 20, 84, 141, 146
Compliments, 96
Conflict, 73
Contracts, 68–71
Control trips, 58–60, 182
Cousins, Norman, 188, 191
Critic, see Subpersonalities
Cuber, John, 82

Dante Alighieri, 131
Dass, Ram, 140, 148, 205
Daydream junkies, 21–22, 46
Death, 194–201
    fear of, 195
    survival of personality after, 199
Dying, art of, 204–06
de Becker, Raymond, 131
Demands, 64–68, 73, 77, 86
Dement, William C., 116
de Quincey, Thomas, 131
Dieting, see Eating
Disaster fantasies, 17
Disidentification, 37–39, 145, 159, 177
The Dream Game, 123

Dreams, 80, 115–37, 183
   incubation of dreams, 132
   lucid dreams, 129
   mandala dreams, 135
   nightmares, 64–65, 125–26
   recall of dreams, 116
   repetitive, 127–28
   symbols in dreams, 120–25, 135
   warning dreams, 118–20, 123, 125
Dream Sender, 124, 125, 129–133

Earthquake, 17
Eating, 95–96, 119, 144, 172–77
Edison, Thomas A., 182
Einstein, Albert, 111, 182
"Energy follows thought", 14, 59, 187–88, 198–99
Epictetus, 199, 206
Epidaurus, 132
l'espirit de l'escalier, 22, 54
Evening Review, 23, 88, 133
Exercise, 179–80
Exhaling, 164–68
Expectations, 52–3, 61–71, 77, 198–99

Fantasy, 38–49, 105–07, 209–10
Faraday, Ann, 123
Faust (Goethe), 131
Fear of Flying, 93
Female Eunuch, 57
Feminism, 11, 80
Food, 95, 168–77
Forgiveness, 89–91
Franklin, Benjamin, 168
Freeway Blanking Out Syndrome, 16–17, 199
Freud, Sigmund, 27, 82, 115, 120
Friedman, Meyer, 189
Fromm, Erich, 91
Future Prediction, 19

Galen, 191
Gerbner, George, 17
Gibran, Kahlil, 207
Goethe, Johann Wolfgang von, 131
Goodenough, D.R., 116
Grant, Ulysses S., 112
Greene, Gael, 84
Greer, Germaine, 57
Gray Panthers, 111
Grief, 206–07
Gross, Larry, 17
Grounding, 22, 46, 125
Gurdjieff, George Ivanovich, 10
Gurus, 146–47

Hanh, Thich Nhat, 26
Happiness, 53–56, 81, 160
Harroff, Peggy, 82
Head chatter, 23–24, 151
Health, physical, 97, 140, 144, 163–93
Heart attack, personality types, 189–91
Heine, Heinrich, 131
Helpless-hopeless thinking, 191–92
Heraclitus, 56
Herrigel, Eugen, 149
Hesse, Hermann, 106
Holmes, Thomas H., 185
Holocaust, 121
Hospice movement, 205–06
Howe, Elias, 131
Humphreys, Christmas, 138, 146
Huxley, Aldous, 25, 204
Huxley, Laura Archera, 204
Hyperventilation, 167
Hypoglycemia, 169–71, 177

The Idyll of the White Lotus, 52
If-Only-I-Had Game, 18, 22, 56, 206
Illness, 59, 119, 163, 183–84
In and Out the Garbage Pail, 100
Individuation, 133–35
Insomnia, 180–83
Intuition, 75–76, 94
Irridescence, 147–48
Island, 25, 204
Istiqâra, 132

Jack stories, 13, 22
Jaws, 17
Jealousy, 78–80
Jenks, Kathleen, 119
Jones, Hardin, 179
Jong, Erica, 93
Joseph (Bible), 115
Journal, 12, 80, 92–98, 117, 133, 173, 183
Jung, C.G., 111, 119, 133–34, 136, 147

Kegel, Arnold, 83
Kegeling, 83
Kekulé, August, 131
Kleitman, Nathaniel, 115
Kramer, Joel, 77
Krishnamurti, 10
Kubla Khan (Coleridge), 131
Kuhn, Maggie, 112

"the lady with the braid", 84–85
La Fontaine, Jean de, 131
Lakein, Alan, 209
Lao Tsu, 10

LeShan, Lawrence, 138, 141, 191
Letters-that-never-get-mailed, 95
Loewi, Otto, 131
Loneliness, 84–85
Los Angeles (magazine), 172
Love, 88–91
LSD, 204

Madonna, 141
Maharshi, Ramana, 145, 147
MANAS, 99
Mantra, 145–46
Marcus Aurelius, 13
Mathews-Simonton, Stephanie, 188
Mead, Margaret, 70
Meditation, 138–49
    concentration, 140
    detours, dangers, delusions, 145–47
    positions in, 140
    Contemplation of an Object, 141
    Breath Counting, 142
    Breath Mindfulness, 142
    What's Going On at My Nostrils?,
        143
    Mindfulness Meditation, 143
    A Few Hours of Mindfulness, 144
    Meditation with a Mantra, 144–45
    The Who-Am-I? Meditation, 145
Methodist Hospital of Indiana, 205
The Miracle of Mindfulness, 26
Moody, Raymond, 199, 208
Moral indignation, 61–62
Mossadegh, Mohammed, 133
Mourning, 206–07
Mozart, Wolfgang Amadeus, 131

Neighbors-are-watching, 20
Nostalgia sex, 87
Nin, Anaïs, 95, 98

Object-centered viewer, 161–62
Objective Observer, 25, 100, 114, 143
Orgasm, sexual, 80–84

Pain relief, 205
Pálos, Stephan, 192
Peak experiences, 44, 187
Perls, Fritz, 27, 100, 115, 118, 120, 122
Phipps, Joyce, 206
Plato, 134
Poe, Edgar Allan, 131
Pointing-the-Finger-at-the-Other, 18
Previn, Dory, 84
Projection, 78–80, 134, 147
Psychosomatic illness, 95–100, 183–89
Psychosynthesis (Assagioli), 37

Quakers, 89

Rahe, R.H., 185
Rajneesh, Bhagwan Shree, 82
Reassurance sex, 87
Reed, Henry, 132
REM (rapid eye movements), 58–59, 115–
    16
The Republic, 134
Requests, 64–74
    conflicting, 73
Retirement, 107
Rilke, Rainer Maria, 60
Ringsdorf, W.M., Jr., 170
Roof, Simons, 139
Roots, 121
Rosenman, Ray, 189

Saboteurs, see Subpersonalities
St. Christopher's Hospice, 205
Saint-Saëns, Charles Camille, 131
Samuels, Mike, 193
San Francisco State College, teachers'
    strike at, 95
San Francisco Sexual Trauma Center, 36
Saunders, Cicely, 205
Schachtel, Ernest, 160
Schumann, Robert Alexander, 131
Security, 56–58, 86, 206–07
Self-fulfilling prophecy, 14, 110
Self-inquiry, 145
Self-observation, 10, 15, 19, 25, 30, 48–
    49, 53, 63–64, 77–78, 80, 84, 85–86,
    88, 90–91, 97–98, 100, 107, 129, 138–
    39, 141–45, 160, 177–79, 180, 187,
    200, 204, 205, 207, 208, 209, 210
Self-therapy, 9–10
Self-torture trips, 17–21, 49, 53, 69, 94–
    95, 181, 206

Senoi (Malaysian tribe), 126–27, 129
Sensory awareness, 151–56
Sentimental memory game, 21, 30, 206
Sermon on the Mount, 66
The Seventh Seal, 197
Sex, 77, 80–88, 170, 177, 184
Sexual Trauma Center, San Francisco, 36
Shadow side, 62, 80, 134, 147
Sherfey, Mary Jane, 83
Shining side, 147–48
Silva Mind Control, 193
Simeons, A.T.W., 183, 184
Simonton, Carl, 188, 191
Sleep, 180–83
Smoking, 96–97, 173–74, 177–79

Social Readjustment Rating Scale, 185–86
Socrates, 10, 55, 58, 183, 194
Stanford University Sleep Disorders
    Clinic, 180, 182
Steinmetz, Charles Proteus, 182
Stewart Kilton, 115, 127
Stoddard, Sandol, 205
Stress, 139, 183–87, 189
Subject-centered viewer, 161
Subpersonalities, 26–39, 78, 95, 97, 125,
        129, 141, 180, 182, 183, 187
    critics, 19, 22, 27, 33, 49, 130, 156,
        172, 176, 205
    overeating, 176–77
    saboteurs, 34–39, 50, 63–64, 117, 183
    scoundrels, 62
    topdogs, 27, 33, 100
    victims, 35–39, 50, 63–64, 100, 206
Sugar, 169–70
Suicide, 199, 207–09
    threatened, 60
Sweat, 180

Television viewing, 17
Therapy, usefulness of, 10, 74, 75, 79,
    121, 123, 192
Thurber, James, 21
Tibetan Book of the Dead, 204
Time, awareness of, 150, 160, 189–90

Tolstoy, Count Leo, 131
Topdog, see Subpersonalities
Twain, Mark, 112
Two Magic Questions, 11, 25, 73, 182

Unconditional Love, 88–91
Unfinished Business, 62–63, 69, 127–28,
    206

van der Post, Laurens, 134
Van Eeden, Frederick, 129
Van Gogh, Vincent, 131
Victims, see Subpersonalities
Visiting Field Anthropologist, 62
Visualization, 39–41
Voltaire (François Marie Arouel), 131

Wagner, Richard, 131
Weingarten, Violet, 97
The Well Body Book, 193
West, Jessamyn, 77
White, E.B., 192
Wilde, Oscar, 150
Wise Old Person, 135, 202–03

Yeomans, Tom, 28

Zen in the Art of Archery, 149